BOARDROOM BLUEPRINT

BOARDROOM BLUEPRINT

BOOST YOUR CAREER WITH A BOARD SEAT IN 60 DAYS

Callum Laing

To find out more about our authors and books visit:
www.intellectualperspective.com

Contents

Praise for Boardroom Blueprint

One of a Kind. 'Boardroom Blueprint' is one of the most insightful books I have read on the topic. Smart, funny, practical and experience-based. Its no nonsense and structured approach plants solid foundations for any board member wannabe. It truly spurs you into action... off now to post on my LinkedIn profile!

– Marianne Abib-Pech, Author of the Financial Times Guide to Leadership, General Partner - Transitions First

Callum has created a book which provides deep insights into the mysterious process of landing a seat on a Board of Directors. He has a personal, engaging style that makes you feel the two of you are having a discussion over a coffee. In the short time that I have been reading 'Boardroom Blueprint' it has accelerated my own path so much that I am having conversations with three different founders about board roles.

– David Hermann, Managing Principal, Hermann Group

At last a book that demystifies the boardroom! This book has really re-ignited my board journey through its practical, realistic and step by step approach. I was already having conversations before I'd finished it!

– Dr Emma Williams, Director, EJW Solutions Limited

This book is a treasure trove of actionable insights for aspiring board members. Whether you're a seasoned executive or just starting your journey, Callum lays out a clear roadmap with practical steps to navigate the complex world of board nominations and secure your dream seat.

– Keson Lim, Partner, Heritage Ventures

After 50 years of C-Level activity in start-ups, private companies, and public companies in Europe, Australia and New Zealand, I have learned enormously by studying this book, its many pearls of wisdom, nuggets of truth and pure diamonds of inspiration. I will be recommending this book as essential reading for all directors, aspiring, accomplished and well seasoned; there is useful learning, at all levels.

– Greg Eaton, CEO, Board Member, Board Advisor -various

I loved how the book started right to the action, putting me in the shoes of my future self as a board member. It gives clear actionable steps on what to do to go from no experience to a PLC board seat, and how to become a great board member.

– Nuno Vaz, Partner, Innov Consulting

This book not only broadened my professional outlook but also inspired immediate action, leading me to establish advisory boards for three companies.

– Vilmos Somogyi, CEO / ALAS doo

Callum is focused on delivering value in everything he does - a true statesman of business. 'Boardroom Blueprint' finally opens the door to the boardroom. Something previously unattainable, until now.

– Brandon Lipman, Director / Marina Bay Capital

This book demystified the idea of board membership in a short time. I couldn't put it down. In fact, I put together my first advisory board offer before I was halfway through the book. Actionable! Focused! Excellent!

– Dave Wakeman, Principal, Wakeman Consulting Group

Written with insight, in a style that is easy to absorb and action. A day's reading setting up a lifetime of opportunity.

– Ian Digman, MD Racing Line Consulting

Callum Laing is the King of Demystification. His latest book outlines a very realistic path to achieve what is considered by most to be beyond reach.

– Jean-Noel Willk, Retired Vice President, Materials & Purchasing at Dassault Falcon Jet

Who is Callum Laing?

It was 3 a.m. in New York and the head of Nasdaq had been woken up to call and personally apologise for a critical mistake they had made on the day we were supposed to take our company public. The freshly popped champagne was slowly going warm and flat as the discussion moved from 'How could this happen?' to 'How do we tell the market?'

The rest of the day was a blur of PR consultants and phone calls with friends, family and investors. Mostly investors. Wanting to know how this had happened and when could they get their money back? I didn't have a lot of answers.

That was my first day as a 'grown up' public company board director. Over the next year we would create more than $250mn in shareholder value as one of the fastest growing small cap stocks in Europe, be attacked by international white-collar criminals and see a lot of that shareholder value destroyed again, before ultimately having to step off the board and rebuild from scratch.

Well not quite from scratch. Lessons were learnt and over the next few years I would be involved in more than 100 mergers and acquisitions (M&A), most of which ended up becoming public companies around the world that my team and I had set up and managed.

Through that time I sat on multiple boards. Sometimes as CEO, sometimes as Chair, and sometimes behind the scenes as an advisor. In these roles I also got to spend time with multiple other board members and I started to see that in many cases boards weren't quite as clever and sophisticated as I had been led to believe.

I was certainly not destined to be what you might think of as a 'traditional board member'. In fact, I'm probably still not. I was not academically inclined. A decade or more of school reports could basically be summed up in five words: 'bright, but lazy and disruptive'.

What I did have, outside of school, was a work ethic, presumably from my mother who had the unenviable task of raising me alone. From paper rounds to car washing to restaurant kitchens and working in retail, and always with little side hustles to try and make more money. It was probably inevitable that I would end up as an entrepreneur.

My first 'real' business venture was a recruitment/consultancy in the Netherlands at the height of the dot-com boom. It was good timing and good times. Until the bubble popped.

I would spend the next decade or so starting new businesses, mainly in Asia, hoping to recatch that lighting in a bottle. I had some success, but still a lot to learn.

Recently, after 25+ years of building companies as an entrepreneur and fascinated by the intersection of business and investors, I started to realise that there was a very exciting opportunity to help boards by putting more 'non-traditional' people on them. And I thought I would start with getting you a board seat.

I wrote this book so that you could get your first board seat. If other people read it and apply the lessons too that is fine, but I can assure you this book was definitely written with you in mind.

Read it, take action, connect with me and tell me what board you've joined. I know you can do it. I know it can be the most consequential thing you ever do in your career. Don't let me down.

Introduction

The night before the board meeting you meet for dinner with the other board members. Each one of them impressive figures within the business world. One of the newer members on the board, a successful entrepreneur who has just launched a new product to critical acclaim, comes across and thanks you for the introduction you made to an investor that backed her.

You sit next to one of the few remaining original board members, the head of the Family Office who is the biggest investor in this company. Immediately they mention to you they have an idea about potentially buying another company you sit on the board of and would like to feel you out on the idea. You hear them out as you enjoy the delicious starters, waiting for the all-important number that would determine whether or not you will be presenting this proposal to the CEO. When the number comes, you politely explain that whilst the idea makes a lot of sense the commercials would need a fresh look before you could pass it on.

As the other board members catch up and share stories, eventually the subdiscussions die down and the table begins to discuss tomorrow's board meeting. Fortunately most items on the agenda are not too contentious, the company is delivering results and the new CEO appears to be getting the job done. Of the eight items on the agenda tomorrow, only one causes any disagreement. You have spoken to all the directors individually in the past week and you know each side's arguments and you know this particular issue is not going to be solved before dessert comes so you allow yourself to zone out of the conversation and reflect on the journey that got you here.

A recent business profile in an industry magazine had waxed lyrical about how you had always had 'leadership within you' but that in recent years had 'come from nowhere to be rubbing shoulders with some of the biggest captains of industry and most influential investors in the country'. The report wasn't wrong. Two years ago, no one, much less yourself, could have imagined that you would be sitting in this situation. Helping shape strategies for incredible businesses. Meeting and connecting with genuine business titans and being rewarded for your efforts with more money for 'part-time' board roles than you used to be paid for your full-time role. Plus, in the past year you had been involved in a deal that had resulted in you earning significant shareholdings in the company. But even that paled in comparison with what you were going to announce to the board later this evening.

And it all started with a book.

This book.

***

This book is intended to be the blueprint to that destination. It is not a 'guide to boards'. I don't go in-depth into the intricacies and best practices of corporate governance (in fact, I'll explain why it's possibly the least valuable knowledge you need in the beginning!).

This book is purely about the steps that you can take to get your first board seat. And then how you can leverage that to get your next one. Whether you're an employee or an entrepreneur, I believe getting a seat on the board can be a catalyst in your career and fast track you to success.

It is a blueprint that has been used by people in their 20s up to people over 70. People who are minorities. People that are differently abled. And numerous others that believed, usually rightly, that the deck was stacked against them.

The one thing they all had in common was the ambition and drive to apply the ideas outlined in this book.

This Blueprint is not just theory. It has been widely applied across multiple industries and countries. If you have the ambition and are willing to follow these steps then I am absolutely certain you will find yourself with a well-paid board seat much sooner than you ever expected. In fact you might be able to finish this book, pick up the phone and secure yourself a board seat immediately. But definitely you could do so within 60 days of finishing this book.

Why am I writing this?

Well mostly because I knew you were looking for it, but apart from that I was getting increasingly frustrated with the status quo. Although as a species we have made incredible progress, we have also got ourselves into a bit of a pickle and there are still quite a few issues that we rather need to sort out. I'm afraid our governments, left to their own devices are probably not the ones that are going to do it. And that leaves private enterprise.

Fortunately, and probably not surprising for someone who has been starting business ventures from a young age, I tend to believe that entrepreneurs have the best shot at solving the problems and increasing the standard of living for everyone. But they can't do it alone.

Ambitious entrepreneurs who are successful become small businesses which become big businesses, and big businesses tend to naturally atrophy. Boards should be there to keep them focused on the important issues, and protect the interests of all stakeholders. Are the current lot doing a good job of that? Let's just say there is a lot of room for improvement. There seems to be a lot of protecting self-interests and enriching themselves in the short term instead of making the hard decisions that are needed.

More importantly, I think, given the right tools and the right understanding of the job, you and your ideas could be what the next generation of businesses need. My hope is that you will take what you learn in this book, and not just get a board seat, you will become a great board member. A board member willing to put the needs of all stakeholders above their own self-interests. And I think if we can have thousands of companies all around the world with great board members on them who are willing to play a bigger game, that can make a huge difference to some of the biggest issues humanity faces.

In 2022 I decided to set up a small project to help train people on what problems I was seeing on boards and the opportunities that were coming up. Named Veblen Director Programme (the name inspired in part by the US Economist Thorstein Veblen who identified that as price increased so did perceived value), the programme serves members all over the world who harbour the goal of getting a board seat. I'm pleased to say it has been hugely successful and I'm not ashamed to admit that I have probably learnt far more from our members than they have learnt from me. Their successes are inspiring as you will see throughout this book.

This book is my attempt to distil all that learning, mine and theirs, into a format so that you too can get the same results. But I do have another reason for wanting to write this book...

Full disclosure: You and I currently have aligned self-interest. We both want you to get a board seat with a company. You have your reasons and I have mine. In the last decade my business partner, Jeremy Harbour, and our wonderful team have done over 100 small business mergers and acquisitions (M&A) around the world. Over the next decade we would like to do many, many more. We have helped many businesses to go public, to acquire their competitors, to scale through acquisition.

I would like to think that if you use what you learn in this book to get a board seat then at some point in the future you might want to reach out and have a chat with me. Who knows what great deals we could put together?

As you'll see throughout this book, there's always multiple games to be played once you're on a board, and bringing forward M&A deals is a great way to add value and elevate your position.

Now why are you reading this?

I'm not interviewing you for a board seat, so let's be straight with each other. You're not reading this because you're thinking that what you need in your life are more meetings!

Consciously or not you are probably aware that a board seat allows you to create impact. The bigger the board, the bigger the potential impact.

A board seat is the ultimate in high status career fashion accessories.

On Instagram flashing your neon green Lambo might serve you well. But in the business world, announcing a board seat on LinkedIn carries much more weight.

This isn't just about a high-status flex. Business is 100% about trust and its inverse correlation with time. Branding has always been about trust. Big brands spend millions of dollars to try and get you to trust them as quickly as possible. They do this by associating their brand with people you already know, like and trust. I like George Clooney movies; I've spent many hours watching George Clooney movies. There is no way that after spending all this time together he would lie to me about coffee!

This shortens the time it takes for your mind to believe that they will deliver on their promise. And yes, time is money. The faster they can achieve trust the better.

It is no different for you in the other direction. Career opportunities will only come to you if people believe you can deliver on the promise. How can they get that belief? Well, you could sit down for a coffee (I hear Nespresso is good...) one on one with a million people and tell them all about your values, how hard you work, why your family loves you.

That would probably work and no doubt there would be a few people in that million who would have exciting career opportunities that they could punt your way. Sadly, you wouldn't have time to act on those opportunities because you would be already on to the next coffee and chat.

Fortunately there are other ways. Aligning yourself with something bigger than you instantly infers credibility. Sitting on a board instantly puts you in the top 1% of career ambitious people on the planet. It is still rare and exotic and infers a level of sophistication and business knowledge that 99% of other people just don't have.

Yes it's cool. Yes it's the Rolex or Louis Vuitton of the business world, but more importantly it can save you years of your time as more and more opportunities come to you because you are sitting on a board.

In the past couple of years I've asked hundreds of people why they want a board seat. Some want the extra income. Some want prestige and respect. Some just want to keep learning. Others want to give back. And still others have a cause they believe in and would like to use a board to help further their ideals.

You may discover your 'why' changes over time, but it is always a good idea to be clear with yourself about why you're doing this. Like anything in life worth having, a board seat comes with its challenges. But it also can be rewarding in ways you would never have imagined.

Now maybe you're reading this with nefarious motives, but in my experience those people with ambition, drive and frustration with the status quo are generally looking to do the right thing. I hope one of the things you'll take from this book is that it's not enough just to get a board seat, the job is to be a good, or ideally a great, board member.

To do that you need to operate with integrity and with the principle of uplifting the board, the company, its clients and its customers. This may sound idealist, but I believe you should be an idealist. You will be under immense pressure to focus on short-term profits and that is not to be ignored but we owe it to ourselves, we owe it to our kids, to aim for something greater than that.

Inspire your other board members to think bigger, to aim bigger. Inspire your executives, your shareholders, your local communities. You can make a difference with your idealism for a better scenario than today.

But before we can do any of that we need to start at the beginning.

Whilst I think this book has all the information you need, I'm aware that reading a book can be a great form of procrastination. What I don't want is for you to get to the end of this book and think, 'Well that was interesting. Maybe I'll start tomorrow'. My belief is that if you follow the instructions in this book, within 60 days of finishing it, you should be creating your first board seat. (Yes. I said creating, not applying for. You'll see why later.) To be honest, if it actually takes you the full 60 days, I'll be very disappointed, but I understand some people have other things on their plates.

Throughout this book I am going to include some gifts/tools/bits 'n' pieces for you to make sure you have absolutely every tool you need and remove all remaining excuses you might have.

Sitting on a board can literally create untold riches and opportunities. It elevates the conversations you have, the people you meet, and your potential to create real value and impact. But in order to play the game, you need to understand it. This book is your blueprint.

Disclaimer:

This book is about getting your first board seat and how you create great value for the board and the company. Your first board seat might not be what you had in mind when you picked up this book.

Nothing I can share with you is going to get you your dream board job with Apple or Tesla in the next thirty days, but it is about getting you on to the first rung of the boardroom ladder.

I've been an entrepreneur for more than twenty-five years. I've sat on many boards, public and private and advised on many more. I don't claim to be an 'expert' on the intricacies of board governance, but I do now know a few things about how you can use the system to your advantage to get your first board seat.

The insights I offer will hopefully shed some light into the closed off world of boards and the most reliable method I've found for you to enter them.

This book is divided into three sections.

The three sections are: Great People, Great Companies and Great Investors.

In each section I'll leave you with the 5 components that you need to apply to get the best results. These are the 5 components that you repeat at each stage of your journey.

In the last section I'll talk about where the real financial rewards and influence come from.

$$***$$

As I mentioned, I am not an authority on what happens on the boards of the biggest companies in the world, but I do know exactly how you can start your board career, and throughout this book I am going to share several stories and case studies. You will hear from people who have followed this method to get incredible board seats.

The insights I share come from twenty-five years of working in small business, a decade in the capital markets and more importantly a unique shift that has happened in finance which has opened a doorway that didn't use to exist. A disruption to a system of boards that hasn't evolved much in over 100 years. A disruption that everyone can see, though very few people have yet fully realised the opportunity it presents.

A disruption that is your opportunity to get your first board seat.

A final word of caution: I'm nearly fifty years old, I've had a fair amount of success as an entrepreneur and investor and much of that has come from looking at things in a different way. There will be certain ideas I share in this book that will likely challenge ideas and beliefs that you have become comfortable with. You don't need to agree with everything I say, but I would encourage you to have an open mind to them. As you will see I don't share them without sharing the experiences that have led to the ideas and also you will see countless examples of people following the ideas and getting results.

Ultimately I would like to hope that you will follow these ideas, join one or more boards and leverage those positions to have a more positive impact on the world. If between us we can connect a lot of great people, great companies and great investors, I believe we do a lot of good in the world (and have a lot of fun doing it).

How to use this book

In the Veblen programme I see people come in and take very different approaches to getting a board seat. Therefore I expect you might choose different paths through this book. I have tried to cover everything that you need to know in this book to get your first board seat, add incredible value to the board and then leverage that to a bigger board seat if you choose.

For some people they will read this book once, one idea will suddenly click, they will pick up the phone and get going immediately on their board journey. For others they will read (or listen to) this book, take notes, scribble in the margins (digital or otherwise). Then read it again. They will really need to try and understand every nuance before they take action.

Neither approach is wrong, but hopefully you picked up this book because you wanted a board seat, not because you wanted to become the authority on 'How to get a board seat'. So keep that in mind. This information is a blueprint. A guide to start and build your board career. It can give you the frameworks and language to use to make you an 'insider' but ultimately it is up to you to take action.

Don't use 'needing to know more' as an excuse to procrastinate.

Are you ready?

I believe you are, even if you don't. However, it's irrelevant whether you feel ready. As we will see later, the time to take action is before you feel you're ready.

At some point in your board career, someone is going to convene an emergency board meeting. You are going to have to drop everything to attend. You will be given some news (not normally of the good kind!) and you will have hours to come to a decision that will potentially impact thousands of people's lives. You will not have anywhere near the information you would like, nor will you have the time to get it. The buck stops with you and your fellow directors and no one is going to come in and save the day.

How you act in those moments, how you maintain your cool and get the best out of the people around you despite the scrutiny and pressure will define you.

Reading a book isn't going to make you a great board member. Doing a programme won't make you a great board member. You need to get out there and live it. You need to take action. And you need to hold yourself accountable. Not to me, but to your future self. The 'you' a few years out. Sitting on a board, helping with strategy, growing businesses, creating jobs, connecting dots and solving problems that need solving.

That version of you needs you to read this book and take action. What is the one thing you can do after every chapter that will get you closer to that goal? What is the one thing you can do when you finish this book that will change the trajectory of your life forever? What is the one thing that 'future you' will want you to do as soon as possible?

I can show you the blueprint, but only you can build your board career.

I am unashamedly a huge believer in the ability of entrepreneurs and businesses to affect positive change for the majority of the people on the planet. I'm not naive to the fact that left unfettered, companies can grow out of control and those companies can end up being a net negative on the world as well, but this is where your chance to shine is.

A good board member can help a company grow and positively impact people, but it should also be a moral compass and help those companies to make the right choice for ALL stakeholders, not just those impacted by profits. A board needs leaders willing to step up for what they believe. A board needs people with different backgrounds who will ask the hard questions. A board needs inquisitive minds.

A board needs you.

The Boardroom Blueprint

What is the Boardroom Blueprint? It is a multistep path to getting a well-paid board seat. I believe that if you are ambitious, take on the responsibilities of a leader and are willing to do the work then regardless of your background and current experience you can follow this path to that result. It might be quicker and easier for some than others, but I don't think it's unobtainable to anyone with ambition and curiosity. You will see in the case studies people from a wide range of ages, different races, genders and with disabilities.

You will have many preconceptions of what boards are. You may well have some preconceptions about why you would not ever be hired by a board. I hope to dispel these preconceptions.

At its heart, the Boardroom Blueprint is about understanding the real problems that boards are facing so that we can position you as the solution to them.

Over the years I have had many many applications from aspiring board members who thought that how they had spent their careers made them worthy candidates for a board seat. Sadly, because they had not taken the time to understand what it is that a board actually needs, they would emphasise skills and experiences they had which were irrelevant to the needs of a board.

This is not surprising. Boards have certainly not gone out of their way to make it easy for people to understand what goes on in board meetings, or how you ever become a board member. But until you get that understanding, you can't possibly sell yourself to boards as the solution that you need to be.

The Blueprint has a path to follow but there are also 5 repeatable components that are critical at each step. These are ongoing components of your journey. Repeatable because at each step on the path you will need to repeat the actions that got you there in order to level up to the next position.

The 5 components are:

1. Connections

2. Knowledge

3. Profile

4. Value

5. Leverage

In each of the three sections of the book we'll explore these in more detail to understand them through the different contexts of you, companies and investors.

Just for you

When you've finished reading go and download the Veblen Board Pack. We've created this just for readers of this book as a special gift. It includes several exclusive video interviews with board experts on different topics, it includes your first 30-day guide, what to do when you join a board, a couple of quizzes you can take and some more goodies worth over $1,000.

And you can find it here:
https://boardroom-blueprint.com/boardpack/

PART 1

Great People

The journey starts with you.

What do I know about you?

Let me tell you about the people I work with every day on the Veblen Director Programme and let's see if you can relate to any of it.

They are ambitious and they are impatient for results. Sound familiar?

They get frustrated that people that are dumber than them seem to be further along in their career journey. They want a board seat even though at the beginning of their journey, they are not entirely sure what that even means, but it sounds good and seems like it should be lucrative.

They are definitely not afraid to do the hard work if they know what is required and the rewards are there. When the motivation is right they're capable of focusing relentlessly to get that goal. However, they are at a stage in their career where they also don't want to work every hour under the sun to prove their worth. They would rather work smart to leverage what they already know.

Is any of this resonating?

To certain people, most people in our programme looking to get board seats already appear 'successful', just as some people already look at you and your career enviously. But our members have more drive and determination in them and still feel like they have a lot more to accomplish.

Another trait they all have is a desire to leave a mark, to make an impact, to do some good. And whilst maybe they haven't figured out all the pieces, it feels like a board seat would give them the chance to positively impact more people.

If you're nodding along to any of that then this book is definitely for you.

Some chapters of this book might not seem relevant now, but skim through them. They're useful to understand and you can come back to them as the situations arise in your board journey.

Not only is this the blueprint to get boardroom success, everything I talk about I have found very useful in other areas of life too.

Boardroom Blueprint: do you have what it takes and is it worth it?

Until you fully understand the problems boards face and how you might be able to help solve them, it is not unsurprising that you might question whether you have what it takes to be a good board member.

Part of the problem we have is that because we have never sat on a board, and googling it doesn't really help, it's impossible to tell whether we would be any good. The media and academia only ever cover the biggest, most valuable boards, but that is not going to be where our journeys start. Consequently I find that many people discuss board members with a disproportionate amount of respect and reverence.

Board members become these almost mythical creatures with untold wealth and wisdom.

(Alternatively, if we've been on the receiving end of decisions we haven't understood, our impression of them might be very different!)

Regardless, as you get on this board ladder and start to ascend you will discover that, like in other areas of life, there are some incredibly talented board members, some that are a bit 'meh' and plenty that should definitely not be there. Your job is to learn from, and work with, the best. They should intimidate you and inspire you in equal measure. But that is how you too will eventually join the ranks of 'great board members'.

Right now, you are just 'aspiring' and that's fine, you are at the beginning of your journey and to become good takes time.

But don't let it put you off. No one comes out of the womb as a talented board member. You have to earn your stripes.

No, you don't have decades of board experiences, but you do have something else. You have your own unique experiences. You have your connections and you have your desire to improve. There is no one else on the planet right now that has that unique combination. And even if you're not quite sure how yet, that combination will have real value to a company out there once you learn how to package it. The Profile Component is really where you start to refine your value proposition.

The other way of looking at this will become clearer as we look at what companies are looking for. Imagine yourself as a uniquely shaped piece of a puzzle. Right now there is a company out there looking for a puzzle piece to solve a problem they have. Today you might not be that puzzle piece, but as you learn more about it, you can also shape yourself to be the perfect solution to the problem they have.

The danger, when you are going through this phase, is that it is easy to get distracted by other people's journeys. It is easy to think that others have what it takes and are 'better' than us. But if you're willing to harness it, your inexperience can be more than offset by a willingness to learn and to add value.

I have had board members who think they know everything, and I have had board members who think they know nothing. In almost every case it is the one that thinks they know nothing but are willing to learn and keen to prove themselves that are the ones that deliver the most value. The ones that think they know everything sadly often lack the self-awareness to understand where they could add real value.

This works in your favour.

Imposter syndrome

Ever sat in a meeting and thought, 'Whoah, I'm way out of my depth here. I have no idea what they're talking about'? It happens to us all from time to time and is commonly referred to as imposter syndrome – the feeling that you don't deserve to be in that position. Periodically you will see articles proclaiming the '7 things you need to do to overcome Imposter Syndrome', but to be honest I've never really seen the problem with it. Yes, it's uncomfortable, but that's how we grow.

I started this section with the mantra, 'Get comfortable being uncomfortable'.

As a leader you are constantly going to be putting your hand up and taking on more responsibility even if you don't actually know what to do. That is uncomfortable. You will feel like an imposter. You will feel that not particularly nice feeling. But that feeling is what drives you to learn what you need to learn so that you no longer feel like an imposter.

That feeling is what drives you to become ever better.

And then we put our hand up and volunteer for even more responsibility. Because we're ambitious and gluttons for punishment!

But at a certain stage a funny thing happens. We stop dreading that feeling and start looking forward to it. We stop avoiding it and start seeking it out. At the end of this section I will explain where I learnt the importance of this mantra, but for now you just need to know that being willing to embrace this feeling will already separate you from 99.9% of your competitors for board seats.

'Great People' is the first section of this book for a reason. It is the first pillar of the Veblen Community too. If you don't aspire to be great, you should probably put this book down now. It is easy to find fault in others, it is easy to see what they could be doing better, but until we get comfortable acknowledging our own weaknesses and areas for growth we are in no position to advise others.

Being 'great people' is a never-ending work in progress. It is a personal development journey that is uncomfortable, that pushes us into situations that make us uncomfortable, that forces us to take responsibility for things we would rather not, but yet no one that we consider successful has ever got there without being willing to do the hard work.

Being a great board member always means that you will be a not-great board member first. And that's not fun. But it's a journey. A journey that stretches you, starts to feel comfortable and then stretches you again. If you're willing, the next sections of this book will show you what you need to do.

Finally, although the book is divided into three sections, without the first section the other two sections are redundant. Everything starts with you.

We can look at boards and say that they are exclusive and it is unfair, but we cannot change that which we can't control. All we have control over is ourselves. As the old master Jim Rohn used to say, 'Don't wish the world was easier, wish you were better'.

I don't know what your specific motivations are for joining a board but as you go through your journey you will meet lots of people that have been on boards for many years. Some of them will be amazing people and if you find them I encourage you to do whatever it takes to keep them close and learn as much from them as you can. However, many of them will be jaded and cynical. They either joined boards for their own personal gain, or have somehow lost their idealism for doing the right thing along the way. You may even find yourself on a board where every board member is like that. I would urge you with every fibre of my being to resist the urge to become like them.

Operate with integrity and with the principle of uplifting the board, the company, its clients and its customers. You will attract more people like you and that is how we all win.

A note on wealth

Is being a board member a path to wealth? Well it certainly doesn't hurt! However, whilst the public perception is often that board members are 'fat cats', I know plenty of board members that certainly wouldn't classify themselves as wealthy.

A board seat offers multiple opportunities to create life-changing wealth, but only if you understand the game. In the 'Great Investors' section of the book I will delve more into how you can leverage your board seat to greater personal wealth.

When I first entered this world I was surprised to find that there are many board members who have failed to grasp the opportunities around them.

But like any career move you're not going to start at the top of the ladder being paid millions of dollars a year for your wisdom. You're going to start off sitting on some boards that don't pay anything, then boards that don't pay well. Then pay quite well. Then hopefully upwards from there. What you'll also discover in the third section of this book, Great Investors, is that much of the wealth you're going to create for yourself is not actually going to come from the salary you receive on the board, but from putting together deals behind the scenes. This is where the real wealth lies.

However, to give you some context, your first paid board seat on a public company is likely to be in the region of $40–50,000 per year. That number goes up as the market cap (the value) of the company goes up. Directors of top PLCs can be earning ten times that for this 'part-time' role.

It is possible that, like some of the individuals I will introduce you to in this book, you will take one or two ideas from this book, pick up the phone and get yourself a paid board seat. But it is unlikely. Like most of us, you will need to work your way up to it through a series of unpaid roles. This is the price we need to pay to show we are serious about the role and we understand the responsibilities, but don't worry, this doesn't need to take years. When you have focus and the right frameworks, you can move from free to paid within months as you will see in the case studies.

Timeframes: Everything we talk about in this book, including getting a well-paid board seat, can be achieved in under twelve months, but in all elements, you need to be thinking long term. Part of being a great board member is being able to think long term. To potentially sacrifice short-term gain for long-term success.

This is part of thinking like an owner. A business owner doesn't take the profits from their first sale and waste them; they reinvest in the business and double down on making more sales.

It is difficult to prepare yourself for a lifetime of success if you are fixated on short-term gains today. That is true for wealth, for board seats and even for the relationships you build over the next twelve months. They all can serve you well for the rest of your life, if you are willing to approach them with a long-term mindset. Act accordingly.

The Veblen 5 Component Methodology

There are 5 components that you need to be thinking about at all times. They are not sequential and they are not things you can tick off. They are an ongoing process that is critical to your success. And every time you reach a board-related goal, it is time to go back through these components again.

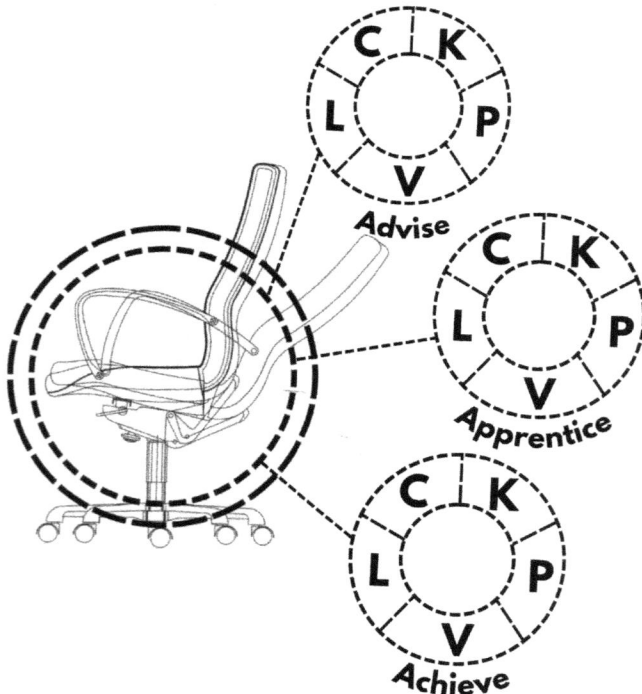

The 5 components are:

1. Connections

2. Knowledge

3. Profile

4. Value

5. Leverage

An easy way to remember this is by the handy acronym CKPVL (sorry, spent hours with a thesaurus and still couldn't come up with anything better!). But if you really want you could try this handy mnemonic:

1. Callum

2. Knowingly

3. Promises

4. Virtuous

5. Lifestyle

OK, maybe not. Just keep this book handy!

We will revisit these at the end of each section to show how you can use them to get results.

Advise, Apprentice, Achieve (and Awareness) – The Blueprint

We have already identified that boards are exclusive and hopefully we're starting to believe that, with the right motivation and some help with understanding their needs, we might be a good fit. But now we somehow need to move from the outside to the inside of this exclusive community.

The problem is when you're on the outside it is very difficult to truly understand what is going on. You don't have all the information or even the language you need and you don't get the insight that insiders do.

It is ultimately that insight which makes you valuable, but you don't get inside because you have insight, the insight comes when you're on the inside. Catch 22?

We need to show that we can be responsible and that ultimately we are worth the big bucks. The approach we teach at Veblen that works incredibly well is that we start by joining, or better still, creating an Advisory Board for a start-up or other small business.

We then leverage our experience there to join, or better still create, an Apprentice Board for a small public listed company. From there we create so much value that we can leverage it into a Public Listed Company (PLC) Non-Exec Director (NED) role.

And from there, we can focus on building the market cap of that company, which in turn elevates our own position, or simply use it as a springboard to join a bigger company board.

First Advise, then Apprentice, then Achieve. Advising is by definition contributing your knowledge, Apprenticeship is a return to cultivating your learning, and Achieve should be a balance of contribution and cultivation through your experience and connections.

Awareness is the final stage and comes from understanding all the games that are being played and how you contribute to them, and at that point you may discover the ultimate irony of board seats.

Advisory Board

Our first step then on this journey is to get ourselves an Advisory Board seat. To understand this better let me explain it from the point of view of the business owner.

My first business I set up with a business partner in the Netherlands. My second business I set up in Thailand where I knew no one. At first it was exhilarating, I had no boss, no business partner, no investors. I had no one to report to but myself. I was finally my own boss!

And I quickly learnt that I wasn't a very good one. I was rubbish at setting priorities and even when I did, I didn't listen to myself. As an entrepreneur you have a million things to do, and if you don't have a clear focus, it is impossible to move forward. I realised that exhilarating freedom was killing me. I was spinning my wheels and not going anywhere.

I didn't really have a good understanding of boards at that point, but I did know that I desperately needed some accountability in my little business. Almost by accident I started building myself an Advisory Board. With the naivety and confidence of youth, I would just approach successful business owners and ask if I could buy them lunch on a regular basis.

Knowing that I was going to be meeting them in a week's time would force me to take actions and try to get results, so that I could present to them over lunch about how dynamic and resourceful I was, and hopefully have something intelligent to ask my slightly bewildered 'advisors'.

Although I was often too stubborn or stupid to take all the advice I was given, enough of it got through that I began to make progress. Today the most valuable people in my network are those I go to for advice about my businesses.

So why would you be an Advisor? Several reasons, but the first is that it's an easy first step that can deliver to you multiple rewards. As you'll see later, the bigger the company, the more they have to lose, the more they will resist making decisions that might go wrong. And hiring you today could be a costly mistake for them.

A small business will often be open to adding an Advisory Board – why wouldn't they, it is basically free wisdom and resources!

Wait, what, free? I thought this was a path to wealth?! Although it's 'free' for the company and you are not getting paid in cash, you will receive something far more valuable.

An Advisory Board typically starts as an unpaid position. And whilst we'll touch on how you can quickly turn it into a lucrative position, even if you can't monetise it immediately, you will still make significant progress in the 5 Veblen components of Connections, Knowledge, Profile, Value and Leverage.

More importantly it will give you the credibility you need to begin your board journey in earnest.

One of the free tests that we offer members of our community is the 'Bored to Board' quiz to see whether you have what it takes to join a board (you can find the link at the end of the book in the Board Pack).

Here are some interesting statistics to consider from several thousand people that have already completed it.

- 1 in 5 people believe that if they just work hard and 'keep their head down', they will eventually get a board seat.

Maybe they're right, but that seems like a big risk to take with the few short years we have on our journey round the sun. Career design always wins over just career desire.

- 4% of people who took the test believed that they should not have to learn anything new to join a board, that the board should 'take them as they are'.

I still find this hard to believe, but given you're still reading, you clearly see the value in learning and, on the plus side, that is 4% fewer competitors for board seats!

- And another 19%, whilst willing to learn new things, would only do so if they were paid for it.

Are you one of those? There are a lot of respected voices out there who say you should never do anything for free as it devalues your time. I often wonder if they would give that same advice to a kid training to be an Olympian? Or an aspiring movie star taking bit parts in theatre production?

I would be wary of drawing too many conclusions from a few thousand people filling in an online quiz, but on the plus side if you acknowledge you don't know everything yet and you're willing to do the work and do the learning before asking for compensation, you are already ahead of 20% of your competitors.

And don't discount the credibility that comes with sitting on your first board. Even if it is an Advisory.

Maybe you've sat on a board before, or maybe you've never even sat in a committee before. People that join the Veblen programme come to us at all different stages in their journeys. Some are young and hungry but with limited leadership experience. Others have been directors of their own companies for decades but have never sat on another board. Still others currently sit on multiple boards but would like to get compensated for it. Or just learn how to do it better.

For all, and for you, I encourage the same path. Your dream board seat might be on a big multinational that everyone recognises the name of, but that is not going to be where you start. You need to learn the ropes, and just because you've sat on a board in the past, doesn't necessarily mean you know how to be a 'valuable' board member.

At its heart the Blueprint is about getting in the door and giving you a chance to shine. It is about creating opportunities where currently there are none. It's about forming a new path, not following what everyone else thinks you should do.

You also want results quickly and that means taking action and going for opportunities with people that can make decisions quickly. The bigger the company, the more the existing directors are concerned about doing the wrong thing.

If they were to hire you to join their board today, it would be a considerable risk for them. They would need to pay you, they would need to give you a vote, and if you don't work out and they need to fire you, it is not only expensive to do so, it makes them look incompetent in the eyes of the market. So we don't start our journey looking for positions in big companies.

We want to start with small advisory positions.

Landing your first Advisory seat and owning the role!

There are two options here. The first is to join an existing Advisory Board. The second is to set up a brand-new Advisory Board for a start-up or small company.

We're going to focus on the second option; we're going to set up an Advisory Board from scratch.

There are multiple reasons why we want to do this, and why you should be able to do this before you've even finished this book.

The first thing you need to do is ignore that nagging doubt in your mind that you don't know how to do it. We'll come on to that shortly. You also need to remind yourself that when you're talking to the small business, you are not doing this for you, you are doing it for them.

Now all you need to do is reach out to a small business. Knock on the door of a small company, a local cafe, a friend's start-up, reach out to a student entrepreneur. For this first Advisory Board it really doesn't matter. Make contact, and offer to build them an Advisory Board for a year that will cost them nothing.

What is the risk for the business owner in this scenario? Nothing. It's all upside. They can even announce to potential clients, staff and partners that they now have an Advisory Board. This gives them credibility. Win, win.

And I don't care how much is on your plate, you can definitely get a positive result within 60 days!

So what is an Advisory Board?

At this level, all we're actually talking about is you and your fellow advisors (more on them later), spending an hour a month talking to the founder strategically about their business over a coffee. That's it. But you get to tell people you've joined a board. They get to tell people they now have an Advisory Board.

Worst case they have to put up with some lousy advice from you. Best case it completely changes the trajectory of their business. Low risk, high potential upside.

And for you, it is the perfect start to your journey.

Let's look at it through the lens of the Veblen 5 components.

1. Connections: You'll build a much closer relationship with the founder and founders are always useful people to know. (As a founder I'm biased, but I'm also not wrong, we're useful people to know!)

2. Knowledge: This is likely the first time you have been able to look inside the workings of someone else's business and start to think about it holistically in terms of shareholder value. This is essential knowledge to develop in your board career path.

3. Profile: The minute the decision maker says yes is the time to update your LinkedIn profile that you are now serving on the Advisory Board for XYZ company. This is important for letting people in your network know you are more than just a pretty face. (And it sounds a lot better than updating your profile to say you're having a monthly coffee with

some people to discuss business.)

4. Value: Whilst you might not be clear yet on how you can add value, that will come as you learn more about the business. Plus I'm going to give you some great tips in the next section.

5. Leverage: You can't leverage your first board seat until you have it. This is an excellent first step on your journey. Your job is to mine it for all the knowledge, contacts and profile that you can.

If you are one of the many people who set up a LinkedIn profile years ago, forgot your password, set up another profile, only log in when you're looking for a new job and think it's full of self-promoting morons then I have bad news for you.

LinkedIn, at time of writing this book (2024), is THE place to focus your time and effort on building your career profile. If you are not already, you need to be scheduling time to post on LinkedIn more than three times a week. We'll get into more in the Profile section later, but be warned, you can't avoid it if you're serious about your career.

'But I don't know how to run an Advisory Board and who are these other Advisors?'

Good question. Being a person of great integrity and a first class student of the Boardroom Blueprint, you know you don't just want to be any Advisor, you want to be a Great board advisor.

Of course we all want to do a great job, but equally we need to remember, because this is a free position, the business owner's expectations are probably pretty low.

This is important because when people have high expectations you can disappoint them. When people have low expectations you can exceed them, and it is the over delivery of value that in time that can lead to well-paid positions.

Low expectations or not, what do you know about advising a small business?

The weird thing about Advisory Boards is that the best ones actually give very little advice.

You can take the pressure off you, and off the founder, by insisting that although it is called an 'Advisory Board' you are going to keep it very informal. It is basically going to be a monthly chat over coffee (this can be virtual coffee – we are living in the future after all).

In the first meeting, you are going to ask them to share with you their business, their challenges, their hopes and dreams.

After that you are basically going to do the following:

1. Coach. Ask smart questions. Why are they doing things the way they are? If they were to start from scratch tomorrow, would they do it the same way? Why/why not?

   Learning to coach takes time, but the better you become at asking questions the better your 'advice' becomes, basically because you help them arrive at their own decisions. A founder rarely gets a chance to talk candidly. To their clients and to their team they must always be positively selling a vision. Your job is to offer them an environment where they can candidly open up to you.

2. Accountability. Have you done X that you wanted to do? Why not? What needs to change? What will you have done by our next meeting that will have moved the business forward?

   One of the reasons that many people become entrepreneurs is that they don't like the constraints of working for someone else. However, like myself, once those constraints are removed they find it difficult to focus. There are so many things they could be doing as an entrepreneur. They might push back on accountability at the beginning but this can be the most valuable service you offer.

3. Do no harm. Your words have power.

   The first two steps here have nothing to do with your career background and everything to do with genuine curiosity and a desire to help. Where I see people go wrong, and it is often done with all the right intentions, is trying to offer their own experience in the wrong context.

For example, an HR Manager of a big company decides to join the board of advisors of a small start-up. In their day job, they know how important it is to have robust HR policies and so, in an effort to help, they offer to help the start-up build something similar. The start-up founder not knowing any better and not wanting to offend their advisor goes along with this and wastes valuable time and resources building something that no company needs until it is significantly bigger. 'Do no harm' is a reminder that your advice, whilst well-intentioned, might be dangerous at the wrong time and place. Coaching and accountability can get you a long way with minimal risk to the company you're trying to help!

And all it takes is some smart questions and a desire to learn and help.

The power of your words

I was at the back of an event once, standing chatting to one of the other speakers, a close friend of mine, Dan. He was an accomplished entrepreneur and I had known him well for about a decade at that point. We were discussing the latest media sensation in small business at the time which was Groupon. For those of you who don't remember, Groupon was a time limited coupon that you could buy to use in local small businesses that would give you, the consumer, incredible value and drive footfall for the businesses.

The results in the beginning were amazing and soon copycat versions of the company were popping up in every major city in the world.

An audience member, seeing Dan and me chatting at the back of the event, came and injected himself into the conversation and proceeded to pitch us his version of Groupon. Except it was very clear from his pitch he had no background in business, didn't understand why Groupon worked and his main selling point was removing the scarcity factor (time or volume) which basically just meant he was selling vouchers.

Whilst not the worst pitch I've ever heard it was certainly top five. As I tried to digest his pitch and figure out which flawed part of his plan I should try and correct first, Dan said to him, 'Wow, that sounds amazing! What a great idea. Unfortunately it's not for me, but I wish you all the very best.' And with that he walked off leaving me dumbfounded and this budding entrepreneur more excited than ever.

There are some important lessons here for when you're dealing with entrepreneurs.

Firstly, and most importantly, you don't know the future. Nobody does. There are some truly ridiculous products that have made gazillions for their founders. When I first heard about Twitter, conventional wisdom was that a blog should be up to 2,000 words long. At 140 characters a micro-blogging site was never going to take off. And, if you think that was crazy, wait till you hear about the guys that wanted you to rent out your sofa or spare room to a complete stranger! (Airbnb, in case you were wondering.) In both cases I was so far wrong it is embarrassing to own up to now, but a useful reminder that we don't pick winners, the market does.

Secondly, pick your time and place. My friend knew that this was a lousy pitch, but where many of us would have been tempted to explain to the young entrepreneur everything that was wrong with the idea Dan saw it differently. He had two choices, leave the person feeling better about themselves or leave the person feeling worse about themselves.

He chose the former. It cost him no time or effort and he made, or retained, a raving fan.

Now I know Dan well, and I know that at a different time, in a different environment, he would have been more than happy to share the areas of the model that would need some work and why, but he had the foresight to know that on the floor at the back of an event was not it.

It is very tempting to show how 'clever we are' by tearing down ideas. It's more clever to understand the right time, place and impact our words can have.

When you sit on a board, in whatever capacity, your words carry more weight than they did before. Be wary of how you use them.

Another example of this I have seen a lot of is a board member making an off-the-cuff remark which can cause unintended ripples. In one example a board director made a comment to an executive as a board meeting wrapped up about wanting to see some market analysis. I then watched as this small company almost ground to a halt pulling resources off much more important projects to try and guess what exactly the board member wanted and how they could provide it.

Ultimately hundreds of hours went into producing a report that the board member in question read the headline of and then discarded because it wasn't actually that important and was nothing more than a 'nice to have'. Yes, the executive should have pushed back and got greater clarity, but equally they shouldn't have had to if the board member was aware of the power their words carried. Don't be that board member.

Going back to those first two points, which are basically around asking questions, is why I mentioned earlier that someone inexperienced but keen to learn can actually add way more value on a board than someone who already thinks they know everything.

But what if the founder asks me a question I don't know?

Sitting on the Advisory Board doesn't mean you need to know all the answers. In fact as a board member of any company one of the most valuable ways you can contribute is not what you know, but who you know. If you can introduce this company to potential clients, new staff members, journalists, partners or investors, that one introduction can be worth more than anything else you could possibly contribute. When it comes to answering questions you don't know, it is perfectly valid to say 'I don't know, but you keep running the business and I'll ask around for you'.

Here's an important distinction to bear in mind if you start to question whether you lack qualifications for a board seat: **Companies don't need board members. They don't need qualifications and MBAs. They don't need engineers or HR professionals. And they don't need you.**

What they need are results. Solutions to problems. Your job is to position yourself as someone that can solve a problem for them. As long as you can deliver a result, it really doesn't matter how you got there, or who you get to assist you.

There is a reason Connections is the first of the 5 Veblen components.

Even Google and PwC have dropped the requirement for job candidates to have degrees because they learnt there was zero (0) correlation between qualifications and results on the job.

You have a singular background that has brought you to this place. A completely unique way of looking at the world, based on your own individual experiences, and a chance to help businesses with your genuine hunger and desire to do so. Much of your experience you will take for granted. For example the city or country you live in might seem pretty unremarkable to you because everyone you know there also has that background. But to a company on the other side of the world looking to expand internationally, you will have a unique set of experiences and backgrounds relating to that country that could be hugely valuable.

Forget what you don't have. Focus on what you do have and understand the problems of your target client as well as they do. If you can articulate their problems and how you can solve them everything else becomes irrelevant.

Your accountability

As mentioned above, one of the most valuable services you can offer as a board member, whether it's advisory to a start-up or on the board of a big corporation, is accountability. Holding executives accountable. You said you were going to do this by this date? Has it happened? Why? Why not? What have you learnt?

Some people really struggle with this. If this feels confrontational to you, it is time to grow up and become the leader we need. Accountability is critical in the development of individuals and of companies. It can be done in a supportive or an unsupportive way. I hope you will choose the former. In my experience it gets better results, but accountability needs to be done.

What about you? Who is holding you accountable to your goals? In the Veblen Community we put people into accountability groups who meet every week to talk through where they are on their journey, what their goals are, what actions they are taking and what results they are getting. These groups, when they work well, are an incredible resource that create lifelong friends and allies. But you don't need eight to ten people; you can achieve most of the same results by finding yourself an accountability buddy. Someone on the same journey as you, that you can check in with on a weekly basis, and just get used to asking each other the hard questions.

Remember, you need to get comfortable being uncomfortable. This is such an important topic that in the Board Pack at the back of this book I have unlocked a video from the Veblen programme with Darren Finklestein, one of the world's leading accountability coaches.

Paid to advise?

Remember that the reason that you are doing this is so that you can update your profile, learn some things and leverage them to a paid board seat in the future.

However, the goal is that we have people offering us paid seats. Your objective in your first year on an Advisory Board is to add so much value in your role that when you start talking about leaving and joining another company board, the founder will pay you to stay.

If this is your first ever board role then that is definitely the route I would take. Start for free, create great value, negotiate for pay after you have demonstrated that value. If you can do that sooner than one year, that is even better.

But an Advisory Board doesn't always need to be pro bono from day one. In fact it can be hugely lucrative if you leverage it correctly.

Dr Keith Kantor, who is an experienced entrepreneur, joined our Veblen programme and within three months had joined the board of three young companies. In fact he very nearly didn't join the programme. After watching one of our webinars, he was worried he was too old (I would share his age, but it's irrelevant, just as the excuses you have in your head are). We're both very glad he decided to join.

Keith took the time to get to know each company, spoke at length to the founders and then in each case he made a targeted proposal very early on in the relationship. He knew that he had the contacts and the knowledge that could seriously transform these businesses. He also knew how valuable that is.

In each case he proposed to the founder that if he could help that business to hit a particular revenue or investment target by a specific date that he would 'earn' a slice of the revenue and/or equity in the company. In all three cases the founders were only too thrilled to agree and the deals have been done. In each case, Keith knew he had the contacts and know-how to make the difference and ultimately those deals are likely to be worth hundreds of thousands of dollars, potentially millions.

If you know that you can make an introduction or bring in investment capital or revenue, you can absolutely negotiate a slice of that as part of your compensation.

The other advantage of setting up an Advisory Board is that you don't do it on your own. You offer to bring in three or four other people to help with this. Firstly this is a great, and flattering, way to reach out to interesting people: 'I'm starting an Advisory Board for a cool small business. Would you like to join? Low commitment, just a virtual coffee once a month with the business owner.'

Secondly, this opportunity you have just provided for the other advisors is not only a great way to build a relationship with them, but also means you will be one of the first people they think of if they get invited on to other boards. It is a great way to build deep connections.

And finally, one of the most powerful aspects of joining an Advisory Board is updating your LinkedIn profile to let people know. Up until this point, your network probably has a very limited view of what you do. When they suddenly see that you are now sitting on a board, it will force them to re-evaluate how they see you, and often can lead to other opportunities suddenly coming to you from people who didn't know you were interested in this kind of personal growth.

Do not underestimate the value of your LinkedIn profile. Follow these steps, update your profile and things will start to happen.

If you are brand new to LinkedIn and have zero connections, update your profile and then share with your contacts on Facebook, Instagram, your WhatsApp Groups or even in your email signature. Now is not the time to be shy. Remember we are trying to build trust and reduce the time to board opportunities.

To finish this section, let's come back to Dr Keith. So focused is he on adding value, that he decided to do a weekly post on LinkedIn sharing what he was doing in the hope that it might inspire or encourage others to do more. About four months into his journey the head of HR at one of the biggest companies in the world reached out to him. She had seen his posts, loved his approach, and wanted to talk to him about sitting on the board of their S&P 500 company.

Excited, Keith spoke to them and learnt that the role was not the main board, but a secondary board (big companies often have secondary boards to serve different purposes). After chatting further they were willing to offer Keith a role on this board for $168,000 a year! Now bad for a gent that four months ago wasn't sitting on any boards and was wondering if he was too old!

What did he do? He turned it down. He was having too much fun and had too much potential upside with the small companies he was working with! A great example of the opportunities that can come your way within months of joining your first Advisory Board.

We will discuss the next step up, Board Apprentice Programme, in the Great Companies section.

Stay the course

Earlier on we discussed how important it is to be thinking long term. This is really critical as a board member, even an Advisory Board member.

Another thread of personal development can teach us a lot in this area.

Toastmasters International is a fantastic organisation dedicated to teaching people the art of public speaking and leadership. More than twenty years ago, when I attended, the first ten modules of the programme were designed to get you to the stage of 'Competent Toastmaster' i.e. someone that can do a best man speech without vomiting first, or could handle themselves in a business presentation without forgetting their own name. Two traits I was very guilty of when I first joined the organisation.

Each of those first modules is around the basics of giving a speech and are very much focused on the speaker themselves. How do you structure a speech? Where should you look? Where do your hands go?

Unfortunately for the world, most people who join Toastmasters and reach Competent level never go further in their studies and go out in the world believing they are good 'speakers'.

If they had stayed, they would have learnt that actually a great speaker is not determined by the speaker but by the audience. Who are you speaking to? What is their objective? How do you want them to feel? What action would you like them to take?

Hence you and I are subjected to many tedious business presentations by individuals more interested in showing us how clever they are than actually understanding and trying to help us.

Sadly I have noticed a version of this with a small percentage of people looking to become board members too and I urge you not to follow the same path.

As you'll see, by following the first three components outlined in this book (Connections, Knowledge, Profile) it is relatively easy to secure your first board seat, potentially several, potentially quite lucrative ones. You may at that point think 'job done – I'm a board member'. But the world doesn't need more bad board members; we have plenty. What the world needs is good, action-orientated board members with a moral compass and an understanding of stakeholders needs. This only happens when you understand Value. What is shareholder Value? What other stakeholder Values do I need to consider?

Without truly understanding Value, you can never move to Leverage. Leverage is the next level up. It is where you can transform your personal wealth, but it is also where you can start to make a real difference for the businesses you're working for and the causes you believe in.

Sadly, you can't be a great board member until you've been a bad board member, but that doesn't mean you need to stay a bad board member for longer than necessary. Stay the course and learn about Value and Leverage. That is where the real rewards lie.

Ditching entitlement: The owner's manifesto for board, and life, success

Consumers feel entitled. When their favourite show finishes, when their favourite product changes, there is outrage and the company is blamed.

Employees go from feeling grateful and excited about a new job to quickly feeling that they are owed this job and if it is taken away then the company owners are in the wrong.

Company owners also make this mistake, they believe customers need their product, are 'brand loyal', but they can quickly have this belief challenged when a cheaper, better competitor comes along.

And investors can also fall into this trap by believing that because they have invested in a company the value of those shares should only go up.

Clearly not all of the players in that ecosystem can be right. An entitled mindset quickly moves to a victim mindset and, whilst that might make people feel smugly sorry for themselves for a while, it doesn't actually move you forward. Part of getting ahead in this game is going to be thinking about things in a different way. Thinking like an owner.

Thinking, and more importantly, acting like an owner is a critical mindset you are going to need to develop as a board member. Sadly, you will find that many people around you will not; they will quickly default to victim, looking to absolve themselves of responsibility and find someone to blame. A key part of leadership is being willing to take ownership, not just for your own issues but for others' too.

Employees will blame you when times are tough, shareholders will blame you when the stock goes down, the media will criticise you because of something someone else on the board does. It's not fair, it doesn't feel good, but if you want to be a great board member, you cannot default to blaming others and playing the victim.

If you want the rewards, you need to be willing to accept some blows below the belt.

Although you may be an unpaid advisor as this point, you still need to think like an owner. You also need to remember that each position you take is just a stepping stone to a bigger opportunity.

It is a great way to gain some knowledge (about the company, the industry, entrepreneurship etc.). It is a great way to make new connections and it is a great way to build profile.

You also need to be aware of some of the challenges that come with the role.

Why do you think this company offered you this role?

The truth is that the founder is likely using you! They have their own hopes, dreams and goals just as you do and right now you are an opportunity to help them get there faster.

Of course they are going to try and maximise this. Of course they are going to test the boundaries of what you can do for them. And if you were a shareholder in their company, you would expect them to do just that. To them you are just an additional resource.

Obviously the better a job you do for them, the more value you provide, the more you should also get out of it. But remember:

1. It is up to you to leverage this position, not them.

2. It is up to you to manage your time and expectations, not them.

If you find that you are giving up too much of your time, talk to them and scale back. If you find you are not being utilised enough, talk to them and explain what more you can be doing.

Either way it's on you. If you find yourself blaming the company for asking too much or not asking enough, you have missed the point of the exercise.

And remember to have fun! This is a game. If a free advisory role to a start-up is stressing you out, you're going to find it very hard to play the bigger games.

Nobody said success was easy.

Which brings us to Ralph White. Ralph is a small business owner in the US. He joined the Veblen Community and then joined the Apprentice Board of a small European listed company. He then secured a paid board seat in the US of a major sports and entertainment listed company. All of this within nine months. Ralph generously shares his knowledge on Advisory Boards in LinkedIn webinars.

Deeper dive: Ralph White from sales to strategic governance

Ralph's career spans sales to board roles, beginning in Memphis and continuing in Atlanta. He has diverse sales experience, including selling vacuum cleaners. Ralph is currently the training director at Elavon, part of US Bank, and co-owns a coffee shop with his wife. He's interested in AI applications in business and has transitioned to board positions, starting with a state charter school board and joining the Private Directors Association. Ralph's journey is characterised by continuous learning and seizing diverse opportunities.

Ralph's first board position was with a state charter school board. Here, he dove into learning about finance and governance. He believes his involvement was a masterclass in boardroom dynamics, where he worked out the distinction between board work and executive responsibilities.

His pursuit of board knowledge led him to the Private Directors Association® where they offered education as part of their programme. He strategically sold some stocks to fund this opportunity, demonstrating his commitment to growth. Here, Ralph actively engaged in mock board scenarios, absorbing insights on enhancing shareholder value and strategic oversight.

'I learned a lot from the mock board scenarios. Then Callum reached out and told me that he was starting the board thing for public boards and asked if I'd be interested. I was like, hell yeah. I jumped on the opportunity. I invested in myself.'

Ralph secured his first paid board position with United Express through a connection he made in the Private Directors Association. This opportunity came about as a result of the network and relationships he developed whilst being part of the association. Ralph's proactive approach to networking and his dedication to learning and participating in mock board scenarios played a crucial role in him landing this significant position. This offered him the opportunity to apply his knowledge and skills at a higher level, focusing on enhancing shareholder value and strategic oversight.

'There's a good rule of thumb for a board member: noses in, fingers out. We know what's going on, but we don't touch it. I live by that mantra.'

Ralph is keen to point out that people make the mistake of thinking that all boards want is a bunch of CEOs. *'If you only have past CEOs on your board you only get one type of point of view. **You really want diversity of thought.** You need the person who worked in tech, somebody who was in sales or marketing. You want a lot of different views. You need to be that diversity of thought.'*

Ralph is particularly interested in finding board positions in small- to medium-sized companies, where he can make a meaningful impact with his expertise and leadership skills, aiming to leverage his diverse background for more significant impact.

Great People starts with you

We started this section with Veblen Mantra #1 'Get Comfortable being uncomfortable' and I want to share where I learnt this from.

Arguably the greatest rugby player of all time is the former All Blacks (New Zealand) captain Richie McCaw. He learnt early on that most of being a 'great' rugby player is being uncomfortable. Training when it is still dark, cold and wet and you would rather be in bed. Getting up again when you've been knocked down. Tackling when you're injured. Inspiring others when you can barely inspire yourself.

At a young age he made the decision to go out of his way to put himself in uncomfortable situations on the rugby field in practice so that when it came to the real games he would be 'comfortable being uncomfortable'.

Richie McCaw decided at an early age that he didn't just want to be an All Black (the greatest honour any Kiwi can have), he wanted to be a 'GAB' – A Great All Black and that would take even more dedication and an even bigger commitment to getting comfortable being uncomfortable. Although now retired, Richie holds the record for most international rugby games won: a staggering 131 (he was Captain for 110 of those).

We don't want you to just be a board member. We want you to be a GBM – A Great Board Member.

Fortunately being a GBM doesn't mean playing a rugby cup final with a broken bone in your foot. Or tackling a Welsh International when you've got a broken rib. But you are going to have to do some things that you might not currently be comfortable with.

To get the role you deserve you are going to have to reach out and have conversations with people way more experienced than you. It can be uncomfortable connecting with strangers and it can be frustrating when our plans don't always work. Once you've done it a few times though you realise it's not that uncomfortable and it is the thing that will propel you forward the fastest.

And when you've got the board role you dream of, you are going to have to have very uncomfortable conversations with investors and/or executives. It's uncomfortable telling someone they have lost their investment or that they are going to lose their jobs. It never gets easy, but it does gets easier, and you get better at it, as we do it more often.

As you've seen the Boardroom Blueprint is basically a Trojan Horse to get you into the inner circle. To get you started on the boardroom career by de-risking it for the decision maker (the business owner in this case) and putting yourself in a situation where you can actually deliver real value and actually be evaluated on merit.

We started with Great People because this all comes down to you and the actions you take. Being willing to try some things you've never tried before, to have some uncomfortable conversations and to take ownership for the decisions that have led you to where you are today.

Five components for great people

Veblen Mantra #1
'Get Comfortable being uncomfortable'

To end this section, let's look at the 5 components needed as we get started. These are very much the entry level. We will look at more advanced strategies as we go through the book.

1. Connections

    There is no escaping this, you need to get deliberate about connecting with people you have never connected with before. The three types of people you need to start connecting with are:

    • Investors
    • Board Members
    • Entrepreneurs

    If you have never deliberately set out to build a network beyond your friends and work colleagues, this might seem outside of your comfort zone, but in today's world you can build incredible networks just through social media. The key is to figure out how you can add value to those individuals.

    If it's a topic you're interested in, I cover building and monetising networks in depth in my first book *Progressive Partnerships*.[1] (However, let's stick to one book at a time for now.)
    Whilst there is no substitute for meeting people in person, we want to be thinking bigger than just the people that live near us. The easiest way to get started on your connections is to go to LinkedIn.

    • Make sure your profile looks professional (if you subscribe to my YouTube channel you'll see I occasionally do profile teardowns of our Veblen members which should give you a good start). But have a profile and a relevant banner image. Make sure you update your info section to sound like you're interested in board-related topics.

• Start following active investors, directors and entrepreneurs. Do a search for those terms, see who has posted recently and like/comment on their posts. For obvious reasons, keep it positive – you're trying to start a relationship.

• Start posting. When you comment on a target's post, it is likely they will check your profile to make sure you're not a weirdo. They will scan your profile and then they will ook to see what you have most recently posted about. My suggestion is that you post two to three timea a week related to board topics of interest. The Veblen LinkedIn page drops two to three bits of content a day you can use for exactly these purposes.

Finally, in the Board Pack freebies at the back I am going to include a video from one of our incredible members Mirenda on how she has used LinkedIn to find an unlimited supply of companies wanting board advisors. Remember, you are offering to help the business by providing a board of advisors. You are not asking them for anything.

A note on LinkedIn. *At time of writing (2024), LinkedIn is the place to build your professional profile and connections. I realise that referencing it will date this book and, by the time you read it, there may well be other platforms that serve the purpose better. The key ideas all remain the same and are, I believe, fairly timeless. So feel free to substitute LinkedIn with whatever AI generated flying robot platform provides you access to connections and profile building in the future.*

2. Knowledge

There is an assumption that to be a good board director you need to be a fountain of wisdom. An all-seeing oracle that can share the correct course of action at all times. We assume that someone who has sat on boards for many years must have such wisdom. Of course it is great to have someone with lots of experience, but with that comes a danger that they believe they know everything and no longer need to learn. Many applicants to boards I've sat on spent more time trying to impress me with what they know than actually learning about the problems that need solving.

Here's an interesting statistic for you. Half of all public listings worldwide experience a decline in share price post-listing, never again reaching their initial listing price.[2] That means that 50% of publicly listed directors have overseen the destruction of shareholder value, not the expansion of it.

Technically speaking if you have not destroyed any shareholder value you are already ahead of 50% of directors that do have PLC experience!

I'm being a little facetious to make a point. Don't be intimidated by your lack of knowledge; it will come.

Rather than give you a big list of things to learn, the first thing to focus on is getting comfortable with the language of business. You don't need to be an expert in these things, but understanding shareholder vs client value (which I cover later) and then how to read a balance sheet and P&L are good first steps.

The easiest thing to do, especially when combined with the above, is to make sure you are checking out the top business stories each day. If you can find a boardroom related angle, not just to share but to comment on, you will be learning and building your profile too.

3. Profile

In Connections we are actively reaching out to people. In Profile, we are making it easier for people to reach out to us. If Connections is going fishing with a single line, Profile is like fishing with a net. The more you can build your Profile (as long as your branding is clear and related to boards/business/investment) the more opportunities you will attract.

In the next section we'll look at ways you can start to grow your Profile, but for now just follow the steps above to make sure your LinkedIn is on point.

If you're struggling to figure out what your personal brand should look like, especially if you already have a brand or reputation in a different area, the idea is not to ignore everything you have built up, but instead combine what you have with where you're going.

So for example if you have spent ten years as a kindergarten teacher, you might head your LinkedIn profile with the brand statement that you are: 'fascinated by the intersection of education and boardroom strategy'. Vikki Sylvester, who you'll meet in the Great Investors chapter, started her career in nursing and has gone on to become a board member. Her LinkedIn profile says: 'Working with a fantastic team of small and medium sized businesses in education and health, improving social & environmental value and having a positive impact'.

The idea is that this intersection is where your value lies and makes it easy for an existing board member to know whether they should connect with you or not.

One thing to note. We are all multidimensional, multitalented people with lots of different skills and talents. However, the human mind can only process one or two things easily. Hence you need to articulate your 'intersection' and try to keep at least 80% of your content related to that. At this point in our Profile journey, we just need a LinkedIn profile that clearly defines who we are and what value we could bring.

Aside: The first three of the 5 components all relate to you getting a board seat. As you are hopefully beginning to see, actually getting your first board seat isn't that difficult. But it is what you do next that will really determine your ultimate success in this journey.

4. Value

Yay! You've arrived. You've got a board seat. Even if it is an unpaid Advisory Board seat, this is still a big deal. Congratulations!!

Now what?

You've got lots to learn, but also you want to start delivering value as soon as possible, because ultimately it is the value that you will be paid for.

How you add value will be largely determined by your experience, your connections and your effort.

The low-hanging fruit to start with is following the guide on asking questions and holding the board accountable, then starting to look at your connections for who you could introduce them to. Potential clients, potential investors, other advisors. Become their cheerleader on social media.

Not only is this great for them, it shows other companies that you would also likely do that for them if they were to offer you a board seat.

If you are thinking you don't need to put in the effort because you are not being financially rewarded, you are missing the point. You get financially rewarded *because* you deliver value.

Strikers on football teams get paid because they score goals. But they can't score goals unless they are on the pitch. YOU are now on the pitch. Don't waste this opportunity. It's a privilege and if you don't want it, there are a long line of ambitious people behind you, boots laced up, waiting for their turn in the spotlight.

If you join a board and then don't show up to meetings, or show up late or disinterested, you are draining energy from the company.

If you join a board and don't respond promptly to communications from your Chair and other directors, or requests for assistance from the company, you are not just letting down the company, you are severely damaging your reputation from the exact people who can and will help you most in the future.

You're on the pitch. Go to work. Go score some goals!

5. Leverage

One of the key ideas is that no position you take is the final one; it is merely a stepping stone to the next opportunity. That doesn't necessarily mean a stepping stone into a new business.

It could be that joining a start-up is just a stepping stone into helping that company become a large company. Or maybe even going public. The point is that you need to immediately be thinking about the next steps.

The first thing you will do is go back through the 5 components. You should notice that certain connections now become easier with 'Board Member' in your title. You should also notice that it is easier to reach out to other companies about potentially setting up an Advisory Board for them now you are already on one.

Just because you have got your first board seat, now is not the time to rest on your laurels. It is the time to think bigger and leverage what you have already achieved.

Hopefully you will have also created lots of value for the founder of the company whose board you are sitting on. Once you feel like you have created enough value, it is normally a good time to have a conversation with them about whether it's better to stay as an Advisory Board, or to move to a more permanent relationship as an actual board of directors. If you have created enough value the founder should want to make you permanent, but if you're going to take on the responsibilities of an actual director you will of course need to be compensated for it.

Note: *The number of boards you can realistically serve on and still add value is limited by the amount of time you have. Whilst some people are happy to spread themselves thin, in my experience five is the absolute maximum number you can commit to and three is probably enough for most of us.*

I would rather have three well-paying seats that I'm fully committed to than five or more that I'm not really able to contribute fully to.

---

1. Laing. C, *Progressive Partnerships: The Future of Business*, Rethink Press Limited (2016)

2. Long-Term Shareholder Returns: Evidence from 64,000 Global Stocks, *Financial Analysts Journal, Forthcoming*, 89 Pages Posted 14 Oct 2020 Last revised: 7 Mar 2023 https://papers.ssrn.com/sol3/papers.cfm?abstract_id=3710251

PART 2

Great Companies

Veblen Mantra #2
'Don't apply for board positions, create them'

Unless we decide to spend the rest of our lives supporting start-ups, ultimately we will want to start moving up the food chain and working with bigger companies. Bigger companies mean bigger opportunities, impacts, resources and rewards.

So we probably need to learn a bit about them.

A bigger company is anything bigger than the company whose board you are currently serving on. There are many rungs on the ladder before we end up on the board of a giant company. You can do medium or large; you can do private or public.

You'll find that a surprisingly high number of large private companies don't even have a board, so you can use the same methodology as we discussed in the first section to create a board for them. Once you get into the realms of public companies though, you will find they all have existing boards so we need to look at different strategies.

In the interests of not repeating myself, let's assume that you are ready to start looking at small public companies.

Why the board wants you and the problems you'll solve

The truth is they probably don't. Companies, like people, are mostly happy with the status quo. Therefore you need to present an incredibly compelling proposition that they can't possibly say no to (we'll get to this in the Great Investors section). Or make it so easy and risk-free for them that their only answer can be yes. Preferably both.

When we were looking at Advisory Boards I said that there were two options: Join an existing board or create a new one. But how do you 'create a new one' if they already have a board?

Let's first look at why I'm so against applying for existing board seats.

It's probably because I'm a business owner and have hired hundreds and hundreds of people over the years. I just don't think traditional job applications are particularly fit for purpose. Applying for a job, you are basically lining yourself up in a beauty parade where you don't know what the judges are really looking for. The odds are mostly stacked against you. Maybe you get lucky, but you have very little control over the outcome and I've always found it pretty disempowering, not to mention depressing, to give some HR intern (or AI) that much control over something so important to you.

If you took away everything I had today, I would not be applying to job ads.

> HR Humour: If I have a large pile of job applications on my desk, I split them into two equal piles. Then I dump one of the piles into the bin.
>
> – I would never want to hire anyone so obviously unlucky!

Secondly, when it comes to boards, I'm always sceptical as to why they are advertising. We know boards only like to hire people they know and trust, so if they're advertising there is a strong chance they have already made a decision, but they need to prove a point to someone internally or for some other reason. Either way it's not a real job opportunity.

Alternatively it might not even be a company posting the advert; more likely it's a recruitment company using a honey pot. You apply for the fake board seat, they fill their database with you and lots of great executives, explain that unfortunately the board seat is no longer available and then try to funnel you to other positions they are trying to fill. (My first company was a recruitment company. This is not entirely guess work...)

I've actually spoken to people who know the above and still apply for these board seats. It feels 'productive' to be doing so and then you can go and write grumpy posts on LinkedIn about how you've applied for hundreds of board jobs and there is institutional racism, ageism, sexism or whatever other 'ism you want to claim. You may be right, but sending a hundred applications isn't nearly as productive as learning the system and then circumventing it.

Finally, a board member is a really key role for an organisation. You're not working your way up to the top, you are the top and you should be having conversations accordingly. Conversations at the top do not start with a job application. It is much more akin to a partnership discussion.

When you're on your way up, applying for a job is all about *you*. Will it help your career? Is the compensation for you good? Is it a nice company for you to work for? Will it help your reputation?

But we are future great board members. We need to be thinking bigger than just our own needs and we need to be engaging in conversations about what the company needs, not what we want. You just don't get a chance to start a conversation off on the right foot if you're being filtered through an HR recruitment process.

So what's the alternative? **Don't apply for board seats, create them!**

Just like we did with the Advisory Board, we are now going to look to do something similar with the PLC. And just like before, we are going in looking to solve a problem for the company, not focused on our own needs.

When we speak to the small business / start-up and offer to create a board of advisors for them, we are not only solving a problem for them, we are creating a role for ourselves and four or five others. A role the company probably didn't even realise they needed, but when you do it well they will soon discover they can't do without.

When we approach a small cap PLC we have to do something similar. We need to solve a problem for them, create a role for ourselves and others and do it all in a way that the company can't say no.

It is actually easier to create a role that solves a problem than join the queue of people applying for board seats through the front door. The average tenure of a board member is nine years so even if the job ads were real, we don't want to wait that long for the turnover.

As I mentioned earlier, board recruitment is more like a partnership dance. It should be a meeting of equals, where each party is bringing something valuable to the table with a view to creating something even better.

Imagine a busy entrepreneur or Chair of a board. Every day they're approached by people who want something from them, over and over again, relentlessly. Then one day you reach out and you don't want anything from them, in fact you want to do something for them.

You want to create value for them. You articulate the problems they are facing, acknowledge they don't have the time or resources to solve this themselves and you offer to do it for them. At no cost.

And if they don't say yes, you are more than happy to offer the same opportunity to their competitor.

Who do you think they would rather talk to? You or the person who keeps asking for something?

But what is it the PLCs want? They already have a board.

What problems are you solving?

Of course every company has different problems. Sadly none of those problems is a burning desire to enhance your career, so how do you position yourself as the solution to their problems?

Well there is one near constant amongst 99% of companies in the world and especially PLCs.

As you'll see in the next section on investors, if you had enough money, you could buy yourself on to the board of almost any company in the world. Because ultimately all companies have a price. Which means that even if a company is not actively fundraising, there is a strong chance that they are interested in investors.

For a start-up company an investor can give them much needed capital for growth. For a better established business an investor can allow the founder to capitalise on the value they have created and 'take some chips off the table'. For public companies, more investors means an ever-appreciating share price, and that not only gives a company way more options for growth, especially acquisitions, it can also make the board very wealthy.

In fact for PLCs increasing their share price is normally priorities one, two and three.

So the most valuable solution to a problem all small cap PLCs have is that you can **help them access new or more investment.** In the next section we'll see how you can do that directly. For now, I'm assuming you are not yet connected to anyone who has a spare few million they will invest in random companies just to help your career? In which case we need to get a bit strategic.

And that means you need to understand how to achieve the same thing indirectly.

For that it's time for us to talk about ESG and diversity. Don't skip ahead, this is important!

ESG – Environmental Social Governance

If you've never heard of ESG before, buckle up. Whether it's called ESG or evolves into something else, it is going to be a feature of every board meeting for the next decade at least. Cut through all the nonsense and ESG is just about trying to get companies to do the 'right thing' for the future. Try to keep that in mind as it is very easy to lose sight of.

Let me be clear, trying to understand how all the elements of ESG tie together can be a little overwhelming. I wouldn't even be addressing it unless I thought it was one of the most valuable tools you could have in your arsenal for getting a board seat.

The reality of the world we're living in today is that if you don't understand what ESG is then you are not going to stand a chance on boards of PLCs and increasingly in the private sector too.

I will be the first to admit that ESG is an abomination of a brand. I believe that each element of ESG, environment, social and governance, is worthy and has merit.

Put it all together though and even with the best will in the world you are going to confuse the masses and end up with people pulling in different directions trying to achieve the same goals.

On the plus side, the fact that ESG is such a mess, complicated and misunderstood, means it's one of the biggest opportunities for you the aspiring board member. There is many an existing board member who is completely bewildered by all this talk of ESG and the increasing government regulations, and has absolutely zero intention of taking the time to learn about it. That is great news for you.

So how is this useful?

This book is about how you get a board seat and excel at it. Therefore I am not going to give you a thesis on the merits or otherwise of ESG. There are a million other resources you can google if you want that. (I'm going to include a vid in the Board Pack that will help shortcut the learning for you.)

In this book I am purely going to talk about it in the context of how it is useful for your ambitions.

In a nutshell, ESG really emerged after the Global Financial Collapse (GFC) in 2007/8. Up until then we had built up quite a lot of interest in CSR (Corporate Social Responsibility) i.e. companies giving back to worthy causes. But as soon as the markets crashed CSR fell out of fashion, and it was realised that part of the GFC problem was caused by a lack of good governance in companies. Oh and also the environment is nearly beyond repair, so let's throw all of that into a pot, call it ESG and regulate companies to become ESG compliant.

Now, as with many things, most of these ideas are good on their own, but put together you end up with a bit of a bugger's muddle.

Companies don't exist in a vacuum. They have a responsibility to the society and the world they exist in. And whilst a few companies were genuinely trying to do the right thing, there were certainly lots of companies operating with a short-termism and a lack of values beyond anything other than maximising profit.

Along comes ESG; governments get involved and suddenly companies are under pressure to comply.

Of course there are still plenty of people who don't care; people who just want to get on, make profits, and hope that someone else will figure it out (the end-of-the-world stuff and other problems).

But part of being the leader you are is to keep increasing what you take responsibility for. And even if you had the selfish instincts of a toddler who hasn't yet learnt to share, there is a strong personal financial reason for embracing ESG.

Specifically there are two elements of ESG that you can utilise to get yourself on to, and then make yourself invaluable to, a board.

1. Reporting

2. Diversity

Let's start with reporting and then I'll do a quick section on diversity as the set-up to how you get to join a PLC board.

If, on your board journey, you happen to be in a board meeting where all board members are happy, energised and excited and you're feeling particularly Grinch-like, you can kill the atmosphere in the room and reduce the board to shells of their former selves, just by saying the words 'ESG Reporting'.

Like Superman and Kryptonite, you will see faces collapse, chests sag, shoulders slump and quite possibly one or two board members actually slither under the table. It's remarkably effective.

The reason it's so effective is that most boards don't understand it, don't want to understand it, yet know it is essential and becoming more essential with every passing month.

Governments are requiring it, clients and suppliers are requesting it and more importantly and fundamental to you: Investors are demanding it.

Ta da: Boardroom problem

And where there is a problem, you can pop up as a solution by offering to do this for them. Just keep this thought in your mind for a moment. We'll come back to it. The next key element of ESG is diversity.

The diversity trump card

This may be the most controversial part of the book and yet I make no apologies for it. However, I am going to skip over most of the elements of why hiring for diversity is the right thing to do. Honestly there is so much data out there it should be a no-brainer. There are plenty more qualified people than me to make that argument and I don't think we need yet another white male mansplaining diversity to those on the wrong side of it.

Diversity on boards is a strategic advantage, but it is also a hard sell. Let me explain why it is so hard to get boards to change.

Even forward-thinking boards are reticent to break up the 'old boys' club on the board and bring in fresh voices. And who can blame them? If you've ever tried to manage a committee it is tough to get consensus. One person being obtuse can derail every meeting and slow things down for months or years. So whilst diversity might sound like a good idea for boards, it is no surprise that boards are not queuing up to add new people to the table. To them 'diversity' sounds like 'disruption' and running a board s hard enough as it is without choosing to add disruptive elements.

To this end there is little point telling boards to add diversity. And yet, diversity can unlock big dollars for boards.

Much of the criticism I get for talking about board diversity is the idea that we shouldn't be hiring based on anything other than merit. Whilst this is undoubtedly a fine idea, it overlooks a significant issue: how can one have the opportunity to prove their merit if they were born the 'wrong' gender, the 'wrong' colour, or attended the 'wrong' schools, among other disadvantages? Let's just address the idea that anyone in the past has been hired on merit.

I would argue that hiring on merit is mostly BS. **Boards haven't been hiring people on merit for the past 100 years.** The vast majority of them have been hiring friends, contacts, people that went to the same school, people that can do them a favour back, people that were well connected, people that looked a certain way, spoke a certain way, thought a certain way. People that weren't going to upset the apple cart. Is that merit?

There are definitely some very competent people within that group, but there are plenty more that don't really deserve to be there.

Whilst there have been some commendable efforts to try and change this exclusive boys' club from the top, including increasing attempts by governments around the world, the approach has always focused on the biggest companies. Let's regulate the biggest companies and hope it filters down.

I suppose we could wait for that to happen... Or we could get out and start affecting change ourselves. Whilst I'm an optimist at heart, I have never had a lot of faith in politicians being able to fix the pressing issues of our time. It's a full-time job just getting elected and finding ways to attack your opposition. That doesn't leave a lot of time for actually solving problems. So that leaves us.

Now before you think this book is going to veer off course into a woke ideological tirade on why boards should be doing the right thing, let me disappoint/reassure you.

Whether or not I think boards should be inclusive is irrelevant. They are not going to change for ideological reasons. If we want to get you a board seat, we need to do so because there is a commercially sound reason for a company to take you on.

And this comes back to the very heart of what we're talking about. Understanding the problems boards face and understanding how, regardless of your background or current experience, you can help provide the solution.

By the way, if you're a poor deprived white, middle-aged man, like myself, and think this doesn't apply to you, I encourage you to read on. In the 'small world' chapter, I'm going to show you how you too can use diversity to get a board seat.

The key tenet of diversity actually has nothing to do with demographics and everything to do with psychographics. If a board is going to make the best decisions, it needs to have access to multiple different ideas and opinions that it can consider to pick the best option. Diversity of thoughts, unity of action. So theoretically five men from the same universities, same industries and same country club could have the full range of diverse viewpoints – but it's unlikely.

What brought this to a head is that, in the global financial crisis of 2008 (GFC), investors lost trillions of dollars because all companies were thinking the same way. For the first time in history, investors went from demanding that boards had 'traditional, experienced board members' to demanding that boards had fresh thinking and alternative views on their boards. Investors started demanding diversity.

As I've mentioned earlier, this new governance thinking was all part of the hodgepodge of ESG which became very trendy in investing circles. In fact so much so that funds went out and raised close to twenty trillion dollars into ESG funds i.e. funds that would only invest n companies doing good ESG practices. Like diversity.

Do you see where this is going?

Boards around the world are currently in a bit of a pickle.

1. They all need to come up with ESG reporting and whilst it's critically important there is normally nc one on the board that has any interest in taking on that added, extra, non-clearly defined, responsibility.

2. Companies want access to investor funds, yet ESG funds cannot invest in boards that don't show diversity. And nobody on boards wants the disruption of new potentially cisruptive board members.

So now we have a very clear idea of a problem that most small PLCs are facing. The Advisory Board was a great Trojan Horse to get us on to the boards of small businesses. What can we use to do the same for PLCs?

Mastering the game: How understanding different stakeholders elevates your level

It's possible that in the process of joining small company boards you decide that actually you're quite enjoying it, you're learning lots, you're getting decent pay and enjoying the people you're meeting and helping. If you decide to stop at that point, it is perfectly reasonable. There are plenty of reasons not to want to take on the responsibility and scrutiny that comes with a public board, but if you're committed to the journey it's a step you need to take.

The reason we do this sequentially, i.e. small company Advisory Board before we ever talk to a PLC, is that it is a big step up in responsibility. It is also exponentially harder to get a seat on the board. At least it is if you do it the traditional way.

One of the reasons it is so hard to get a board seat on a PLC is that directors of public companies are often terrified about doing the wrong thing even if on paper you look like a perfect candidate.

Think of it from the company's perspective. Making the wrong hire for an entry-level role is annoying, but it should be relatively easy to replace. In fact high turnover in these roles is very common. Think service staff, customer care, basic sales.

The higher up the organisation you go, the more expensive it becomes when you make a bad hire. Not just in salary and redundancy payments, but in the disruption to the organisation of getting it wrong.

Now the board is of course the pinnacle, and though you might think a board member coming and going doesn't have too much impact on the day-to-day running of the business, it can have enormous implications in public companies.

First off, if the board hires someone new and that person turns out to be a bad fit (maybe they are not engaged; maybe they are actively disruptive), this can seriously hamper board activities. In a normal company situation you sit down with the individual, have the hard conversation, and then ask HR to find a replacement. With the board you need to notify shareholders that you as a board picked a wrong'un.

And the market doesn't like disruption in the board. It makes them nervous, and when they get nervous, they sell. And when they sell the value of your shares goes down.

So then as a board you find yourself stuck having someone useless, or disruptive, on the board for many years. Or having to admit to the market that you got it wrong. Neither are particularly appealing options. It's no wonder that boards only ever hire people like them!

Added to that, if you don't have any PLC board experience, even if you were a good candidate, they are going to have to get you up to speed. Which is why most will always revert to the 'sorry, you don't have enough experience' excuse.

As always, and hopefully one of the key messages you are starting to see, your job is to help solve a problem for the board. And you telling them you have ten years of marketing experience, or twenty years of supply chain management experience, is absolutely not what they are looking for.

But you telling them you can help them with their ESG reporting or with finding new investors? Now you have their attention.

The Trojan Horse we use to get into the inner circle of PLC boards is the Board Apprentice Programme.

A Board Apprentice (you) is included in all board communications and sits quietly in board meetings in order to learn from the existing board. The Board Apprentice doesn't get paid, doesn't vote, doesn't speak unless spoken to. They are just there to learn.

This all sounds great for getting you PLC board experience, but why would a company agree to have a bunch of strangers sitting in their meetings?

Because we don't pitch it in terms of what it can do for us, we pitch it in terms of what we can do for the company.

Let's say that as part of your Connections component, you have been building a relationship with the Chair of a small PLC in an industry you're interested in (you have, haven't you?). You maybe send them interesting articles from time to time, you mention you've even bought a few of their shares, you ask some pertinent questions about the industry.

And then you ask them if they are interested in connecting with more investors?

When you get the inevitable positive response, you can say you have a solution that they might be interested in that won't cost them anything, could save them a ton of work and could bring in a lot of investment capital.

The pitch is that you will build for them a diverse Apprenticeship Programme made of talented individuals from your network who are keen to take on more responsibility especially around ESG reporting and investor relations. Also with a diverse apprenticeship board, you will be able to reach out to many of those funds who can't consider this company because of the current lack of diversity.

The benefit to them is that, for no cost, they now have resources that will help them put together the dreaded ESG reports AND will help them reach out and connect with new investors. What's more, because you will be putting together a 'diverse' group of Apprentices, they can now tell the market that they are taking steps to improve diversity at the highest level of the organisation.

Without having sat on a board and fully understanding the pressure that PLC board members are under, it might be hard to appreciate what a tempting offer you have just put in front of them.

The proposition is super compelling, but more importantly it is completely de-risked. It doesn't cost them anything and they can always change their minds if it isn't working out. (You will make sure it works out!)

Like the Advisory Board before you, this actually solves a very real problem and most importantly gets you on to the inside of an actual PLC board. You are now in the inner circle.

The Apprentice Programme gives you the chance to build your Connections, Knowledge and Profile all whilst providing Value to the company.

Again, because this is an unpaid role, the expectations of the company will be very low. This means that when you do the excellent work of pulling together an ESG report for them (don't worry if you currently have no idea how to do this; you and your fellow Apprentices will have time to learn once you join the board) and introducing them to relevant investors they will be blown away.

This will make you a very strong candidate for a paid role at the end of the year.

One additional interesting point on the idea of setting low expectations. A common problem I have seen in new first time board members is a desire to 'make a mark' when they first join the board. Often this is the most amount of money they have ever been paid for the least amount of time (a board role is typically a one to two hour meeting every month or two – plus reading). Therefore they assume to prove their value they need to come in, sound smart, and try to solve everything in their first meeting.

Without understanding the nuances of the business, the existing politics and relationships on the board or any of the history, they wade into their first board meeting determined to show what a great new board member they can be.

Although well-intentioned, this often means they trample over everyone else and ultimately this enthusiasm to the right thing means that their board tenure is disappointingly short.

When you're a Board Apprentice with a mandate to sit there and learn, you actually get a chance to read the room to understand the real power dynamics within the board. You get to see how it really runs, rather than just what you were told at the beginning. This is extremely powerful information and can stop you making critical mistakes in the future.

Finally, there is one additional hidden benefit to being a silent Apprentice. Most directors hate being challenged in the boardroom; although it's critical to business success, we all have sensitive egos. Even if you vehemently disagree with someone on the board, as an Apprentice you just have to bite your tongue. What happens is that, as the end of the year approaches, many of the board will value you, precisely because you have never challenged them. Assuming your silence is approval of their ideas and thus an example of your wisdom and clear thinking.

Whether or not this is true, it certainly doesn't do you any harm when they come to discuss making you a full NED or not!

Understanding business

If you want to represent a business it helps to understand all business. But this is a big topic, far bigger than the scope of this book. And quite frankly I've been starting and building businesses since I was a kid, and I'm pretty confident that I've only got the hang of about 1 or 2% of it.

But a good first step is to start thinking holistically about a business.

Most of us start off as employees in a company. We get told to answer the phones, clean the floors, sell the merch, respond to the emails, enter the databases or whatever other menial task could get our first step on the ladder.

After lots of roles like those above, my first 'real' job was with a very successful Internet company at the height of the dot com boom. They were growing quickly and they needed helpdesk people. I had some basic understanding of computers, and, although I didn't really understand the Internet (it was still very new at that point), I apparently had a pleasant phone manner and in true call centre fashion could repeat the phrase 'please bear with me' with no loss of enthusiasm whilst staring blankly at a screen trying to figure out what I was looking at.

I was sufficiently good, enterprising and hard-working at this, and the company was growing fast enough, that I managed to get myself promoted six or seven times in the space of a couple of years. I honestly don't remember what my title was when I finally left to start my own company, but by any definition within the European Operations Center I was fairly senior and knew as much as anyone about how to add a client to our network and route traffic around the backbone of the internet.

For this I was extremely well-paid and very much in demand by European telcos who were trying to catch up to this Internet thing.

What I didn't know, and in fact didn't even realise I should have known, was how the company made money. Hidden away in our darkened operations centre we were very much the heart of the business. If something went down, our screens went red and we leapt into action, acutely aware of how important it was to get things back up and running.

But did we actually understand how our business worked? Not a clue. And that didn't seem to matter. Sure I vaguely knew our clients paid us money for Internet services. I understood how the product worked. I just didn't understand how the business worked.

This is the unfortunate nature of businesses. A successful solopreneur has a pretty good idea how their little business fits together. A four- or five-person team might have specialities but should still be pretty clear about what the business is, how it makes money and why each team member is critical to its success.

Grow to twelve people and this is no longer the case. Of course there are exceptions, in each department you will have the curious ones that want to understand how it all fits together. These people usually get promoted to management. But you will find the majority of people are quite happy just understanding how to be the best little cog in the machine without having any interest in understanding what the machine really does, how it does it or why it does it.

When people apply for board seats with me, the vast majority of them explain what a good little cog they have been for the past twenty years. 'An expert in supply chain management'. 'A seasoned HR manager'. Whilst these are admirable qualities, they are rarely what boards are looking for because if you don't understand an overall business, how are you going to help? If I want supply chain advice, or HR or IT, I'll just hire them within the business, not to sit on the board.

Successful entrepreneurs aren't necessarily the answer either. They do have a much better holistic view of business, and by definition they are very good at solving problems. Yet years of focusing on client value (see next chapter) can be a difficult trait to shake. Not all of them have the will power required to not want to jump into the business and try to fix it and that can cause real problems if non-exec board members try and fiddle in the business.

Part of the reason 'You don't have board experience' is such a common rejection is that no board has the time, or interest, to teach you to understand business. You need to have got that before you start applying for board seats.

And if this takes you back to when you were applying for jobs at the start of your career ('how do I get employment experience if you won't employee me?!'), then you are absolutely right. We have come a full circle.

The money is better; the responsibility is greater, but the point remains the same. It's not the company's responsibility to get you there. It's yours.

This is why, whatever stage you're currently at, it is worth beginning your board journey by sitting on one or more Advisory Boards so you can look holistically at the business and understand how it works. This will significantly help you when you move up to PLC Board Apprentice.

Client Value vs Shareholder Value

In my previous books I have touched upon this problem. As an entrepreneur I was so obsessed with 'client value' that I didn't understand 'shareholder value'. At the time I assumed this was a 'small business' issue. Since I started working in the capital markets I discovered it goes way deeper than that!

Just on the off chance you aren't currently sitting with a copy of my previous books handy, let me recap.

Businesses exist to solve problems for clients. That's it. Entrepreneurs see something that isn't being done, or not being done well enough, and, selfless souls that we are, decide to solve the problem better, faster, cheaper and in turn help humanity to live more easily. Whether that is cutting hair better, providing more accurate accounting or designing our AI overlords. And we believe that by solving big enough problems for enough people we will be rewarded. Hopefully richly.

Much of humanity's progress for the last couple of millennia has been driven by this premise.

Fundamentally for a business to be successful, it needs to solve a problem for its clients; this is client value. It also needs to be valuable enough that clients will actually pay for it. And pay a sufficient enough price that the company can cover all costs and make a profit on top.

This might seem obvious, but it is not always. When interest rates were cheap, and venture capitalists (VC) would fund anything (and entrepreneurs had learnt the unhealthy Silicon Valley lesson that you come up with an idea and raise funding before you see whether a client will pay for it), one of the most exciting business ideas was '15-minute groceries'.

Across the US and Europe companies raised millions of dollars from VCs and poured that money into the idea that consumers could order their groceries on their phone and have them delivered to their home within fifteen minutes. What a utopia!

The slight fly in the ointment was that, whilst consumers thought this was lovely, it wasn't sufficiently lovely that they would pay an insane premium on top of the price of groceries. Working on the basis that scale solves everything, the companies subsidised the model by paying for drivers and logistics with the capital they had raised. When that capital ran out, so did the consumers. They just weren't providing enough value to the clients to justify the price increase needed to make the company sustainable.

So understanding client value is critical to the success of a company. Hence our budding entrepreneur who designs a better mouse trap needs to be obsessed with client value. The more value you provide, the more you can charge, the more profit you make, the more shareholder value you provide, right?

Well not necessarily. In our bid to add increasing client value sometimes we overlook what is in fact best for shareholder value.

A client of a small business may want to only be served by the owner. That is excellent client value. But it doesn't scale. Shareholder value is being sacrificed for client value. The reverse of this is companies that prioritise systems and efficiency, cutting costs and denigrating service to increase shareholder value but at the cost of client value.

The irony is that a single founder and owner of a business should understand shareholder value because they have set up this business to benefit themselves. However, because we spend 24x7 obsessing about client value and, without a board, there is no one to remind us about shareholder value, and we often end up making decisions that are detrimental to the long-term value of our own shares.

As I said, I thought this was probably a problem unique to small businesses. However, when I started taking companies public I had to travel the world speaking at investor conferences pitching my stock to supposedly hungry investors.

Whilst I waited for my own chance to get on stage and hopefully dazzle, I would eagerly sit and take notes on the other, more experienced, companies that were pitching.

What I quickly realised was that many of these CEOs, of companies that were much bigger than my own and who had been listed for many years or even decades, still hadn't worked out the difference between client and shareholder value.

More often than not the CEO would get on stage and launch into a product pitch. And often these product pitches were amazing; they clearly knew the problems their clients had and how to solve them.

Sadly of course we weren't in a room full of prospective clients, but the CEO who had clearly successfully sold plenty of widgets with this product pitch in the past had assumed that the same pitch to investors would yield the same results.

Different audience, different results.

Investors want to know why, if they buy a unit of your shares today, someone else will value that share higher in the future. They want to know that the money that they have worked so hard to earn will be safer, and work harder, under your stewardship than if they just put it in the bank. They want to know that their money is safe with you.

Understanding your product and the problem it solves for your market might be relevant to the story, but it is not the story.

Understanding the difference between client value and shareholder value is critical to becoming a Great Board Member.

Corporate governance? Separate the signal from the noise and understand the 5 components of your journey

Search for any book on boardrooms and you'll find weighty tomes talking all about the importance of good corporate governance and what specifically that means. And yet, beyond this chapter I'm hardly going to touch on it, so if that's what you're looking for (perhaps you have trouble sleeping?) then sadly this book is not for you. Before I do this, let me cover some of the basics that you perhaps thought I was going to cover when you picked up this book.

Board Structures

There are all manner of different board structures based on the size and needs of the organisation ranging from the smallest volunteer sports club to the biggest public or private companies in the world. Here are some of the main roles you need to have a basic understanding of.

- Chair (previously known as the Chairman regardless of gender, this is increasingly just referred to as Chair). Basically in charge of the meeting, responsible for keeping the discussion on topic, shutting it down when it's not moving forward, keeping to the time allocated and ideally bringing in voices that might not always get heard to help the whole board come to the right decisions.

- Company Secretary. Typically works closely with the Chair to ensure the board meeting is set up correctly, the right people are invited, have received all the board packs ahead of time, and then records the activities of the meeting and produces the minutes for circulation and approval afterwards.

- Chief Executive Officer (or Managing Director). One of the board's biggest responsibilities is finding, supporting and, when necessary, replacing the CEO. It is the CEO's job to execute the objectives of the board and company.

- Executive Directors ('Execs'). These are directors of the company that work in the business. It is their role to provide relevant information to the board and deliver on commitments. Typically you would always have the Chief Financial Officer on the board to report the numbers, but, depending on the industry, you might also have technical, marketing, sales, operations or human resource execs also on the board.

- Non-Executives Directors (NEDs). These are 'independents' or outsiders who are able to give an external view and hopefully stop the company being too inward focused. A 'pure' independent won't own shares in the company so they can remain completely impartial. Although most companies believe in aligned incentives and would very much like board members to own and ideally be buying shares in the company.

- Sub-committees. Most board members will also serve on sub-committees. These can be permanent, for example, an Audit Committee that works with the auditors to ensure the numbers are right for market. Or they can be temporary, for example, a sub-committee pulled together to help executives evaluate a particular acquisition or major investment which can then be disbanded after the objective is met.

- Guests. These can be internal or external but they are bought into meetings to add colour and insights to information the board needs. It might be a product manager giving updates on a new launch, or it could be a vendor wanting to pitch the board a large purchase. It might even be a member of another company's board coming to pitch an idea like a partnership or acquisition.

- Advisors. Board advisors are as their name suggests. They do not have a vote, but usually have some useful domain expertise that they can share with the board.

- Apprentices. We have addressed these earlier, but they are a way to potentially train new board members. These can be internal or external and can serve multiple roles.

Boardroom basics covered, let's get back to good corporate governance and why, if every other boardroom author is focused on corporate governance, am I not going to cover it?

Firstly what is corporate governance (CG)? Investopedia[1] describes it thus:

'Corporate governance is the system of rules, practices, and processes by which a company is directed and controlled.'

In a recent Forbes article () they pointed to the 'Five Pillars' of good CG as being

1. Effectiveness of the board

2. Compensation and remunerat on

3. Risk and crisis management

4. Relationships with stakeholders

5. Ethics and transparency

The way I find it useful to discuss CG is to look at where it has come from. Think of the life of a business. It starts as an idea that a small team starts to implement and with a bit of luck that company grows and serves more people. In most cases the success at this point has been largely due to the irrational behaviour of the founder.

Irrational because no right-thinking individual would risk the time, money, effort and pain to start a business. To be successful founders need to do things others would not. This is what makes a business successful in the beginning. The force of will to bend clients and staff to your way of thinking.

And yet, this same sheer bloody-mindedness can also cause a great business to fail. Once a company reaches a certain point, making decisions based on the whims of the founder may no longer be in the best interests of the organisation. This is where a board can act as a sounding board. Checks and balances to make sure nothing rash is done. This is all part of the journey of the company.

Now if this company continues to be successful, then eventually the founder will resign / step away from the day to day running. Maybe the company is public, maybe it has got so big it is difficult to find anyone that is accountable. And in these situations bad things can often happen.

In the late 1970s and early 1980s there was a wave of hostile takeovers by visionary, and controversial, entrepreneurs like Sir James Goldsmith who had identified that in the absence of a strong founder presence many executives in the company were basically running the company to enrich themselves at the expense of the shareholders. These 'Corporate Raiders' like Goldsmith would buy up big companies, sell off assets, slash executive pay and return the profits to shareholders. Which was what a business was designed to do – reward shareholders for their risk capital.

This caused a lot of fear and an initial shake up to the way companies were being run. Boards became charged with implementing these best practices to try to avoid outsiders coming in and doing it for them. And yet it is pretty easy to argue that they haven't done a particularly effective job. Executive pay today sits at historical highs, and, whilst more money is returned to shareholders through share buy-backs, it turns out execs who have share compensation often get some of the biggest gains.

And who determines executive pay? See point 2 above on good corporate governance. Over the past few decades, boards, typically comprised of executives, have come to the conclusion that they contribute hundreds of percent more value to the organisation than other workers.

In case that sounds a bit self-serving, those boards will often bring in management consultants for an 'objective review'.

A quick sidebar on management consultants. Like anyone else, consultants need to sell their services. One of the ways they do this is by being an 'external' resource that executives can lean on. 'We don't like to do this, but Boston Consulting recommends we slash 20% of the workforce.' The consultants become a convenient scapegoat to enable big boards and execs to make the hard decisions.

However, consultants needed to find more ways for boards to hire them (there are only so many workers you can fire). So Arch Patton from McKinsey wrote the book *Men, Money And Motivation* published in the early 1960s arguing that executives were underpaid.[2] Executives could now justify their large salaries by pointing to their, equally well-paid, external consultants. He has been credited as a major contributor to skyrocketing executive pay. When asked about it he simply answered 'guilty'.

So if everyone else thinks CG is the most important knowledge for a board member, why am I hardly touching it?

Firstly, as you'll see later, I want you to be thinking International from day one. Although there are many standard best practices for corporate governance, you will find that each resource only focuses on the country where the author is based and the content is heavily weighted to the rules and regulations of that country. Which is fine. But I do not know which country you are currently residing in, and as you will see later I am a huge advocate of going International with your board quest.

Secondly, it's not super relevant. Nobody writes books about good corporate governance for start-ups and small businesses. Why? Because good governance for small businesses is very different from that of big companies.

Early-stage businesses need to be able to swivel on a dime and react quickly to the market and environment. Even small cap companies do not have the resources needed for many of the 'best practices' of corporate governance. It is, by definition, written for bigger companies: 'corporates'. This doesn't make it irrelevant, but certainly less relevant.

Our focus is starting our board career not at the top of the biggest companies, but by getting on the board ladder with smaller businesses. Not only does CG best practice often not work here, it can be actively detrimental to the smooth running of the business. And as we have already seen, one of our core tenets of being a board member is 'do no harm'.

Thirdly, it's worth considering the best companies often don't have the most exemplary CG. Berkshire Hathaway, Warren Buffett's company and one of the most successful investment houses of all time, has a board that is stuffed with his friends and employees. He has no interest in the current 'best practices' that external consultants think should be employed by boards. And investors care not one jot, because he delivers results.

Mark Zuckerberg at Facebook (Meta) has an unreasonable amount of voting shares rendering the board mostly window dressing, and, whilst investors occasionally complain loudly, if they voted with their feet and didn't invest they would have missed out on around 500% returns since IPO.

And let's look at Elon Musk, currently one of the most successful entrepreneurs of all time. Tesla's CG is so bad that eventually the SEC intervened and made him appoint an independent Chair (he was CEO and Chair up until 2018 until as part of a settlement he gave it up), but nobody is under any illusions that Musk is beholden to his board.

Of course there are plenty of successfully run companies that do so using CG best practice, but it's important to acknowledge that a) it is not critical to have it to be successful and b) no company has ever been successful just because they had good CG.

However, the most important reason and the main reason that I'm not going to talk much further about corporate governance is this:

It won't get you a board seat.

This is the main reason I do not cover CG heavily in this book. This book is about how you get a board seat, and how you add value once you are on the board. Whilst it is certainly useful to have someone on, or at least advising, a board on best practice, I have never once come across a company that has said 'Let's hire someone because they are an expert in CG'. In fact the only reason I can even imagine that scenario is if a company was already in significant trouble for egregious breaches and was trying to patch things up.

In my webinar I liken it to you deciding that you want to play premiership football. But instead of training on how to score goals for the team, you instead do a refereeing course to make sure you're an expert on the rules. Maybe it's interesting to do and a nice-to-have especially as you sit on the boards of ever bigger companies, but **the person that knows all the rules will never get hired over the person that knows how to score goals**.

This book is about how to get on the pitch and how to score goals.

Now, I'm not dismissing CG for these reasons; a lot of it can be useful. But I also think that books or programmes that paint it as a path to a board seat are being somewhat misleading.

Types of companies and the problems they encounter

There are 330 million companies out there in the world. And that's just the for profit ones. There are also charities, non-profits, sports associations and others. Actually many small businesses are also non-profit, but probably not deliberately!

Each one of those companies is going to have unique problems. At least it's going to have problems that it believes are unique to them.

What you discover, as you join more boards, is that the problems companies have at any given stage on their journey are fairly predictable. Certainly they have more problems in common than separating them.

When you first sit on the board of a start-up and they tell you that they have $1k in the bank, $30k in payments due this week and salaries due in two weeks, you will be forgiven for thinking it is the end of the world. Certainly the end of their world and therefore the end of your job as an advisor.

But start-ups are scrappy. Suppliers will be put on payment terms; clients will be offered incentives to order and pay in advance; and, worst case, the staff will take a haircut on their salaries until the revenue is flowing again.

After seeing this happen a dozen times, when the next founder comes to you in tears, having not slept for two days, sick with worry that their business will close, you will calmly tell them that they will get through this by putting suppliers on payment terms, offering incentives to clients to pay in advance and, worst case, their staff can take a small cut in salaries until the cash is flowing again.

That founder will leave that meeting relieved and thinking you are a genius.

Each company has its own unique set of challenges at different times in its journey. As you get more experienced you will come to learn these.

A business owner can tell you what industry they're in and what headcount they've got, and you'll be able to tell them their revenue, profit margins, what the biggest internal conflict is from staff and how the CEO is spending their typical day.

Not only that, you will, over time, learn how to tell them exactly what is coming next and how to prepare for it.

To the CEO who is drowning in the business this will seem like magic.

When you're an entrepreneur you feel like every problem is unique to you. As you get more experience you realise this is a well-trodden path which means there are some well-trodden pathways. It doesn't mean it's easy, but it does mean we can learn from others. Our value as an 'experienced' board member is often just pattern recognition.

If you can also learn to interpret the problems and opportunities that businesses of all sizes face and turn that into language investors understand, you will become incredibly valuable.

Deeper dive: Marisa Agrasut's journey to an Apprentice Board position

Marisa is an entrepreneur in Singapore who joined the Apprentice Board of Incergo, a small European listing, and has been a big driver of the ESG reporting. Although a successful entrepreneur and keen to do more board work, she was stuck in the loop of 'do I have enough' experience. Since joining Veblen and joining the board of Incergo, she has smashed that concern.

Before embarking on her Board Apprenticeship, Marisa Agrasut had already carved a notable path in strategic design management and corporate innovation. Her career took a meaningful turn during the global financial crisis, leading her to delve into sustainability and permaculture. This shift saw her developing sustainable ventures in Thailand and Singapore, focusing on organic agriculture and innovating business models. Despite her success, Marisa wanted a deeper understanding and involvement in corporate governance, particularly in sustainability.

The Apprenticeship Experience: Marisa's journey to the boardroom began with a conscious decision. She pursued an Apprentice Board position to gain first-hand experience in corporate governance. Initially uncertain about whether she was ready, Marisa came in to it with an open mind, keen to learn from a diverse set of board members and bring new perspectives to the table.

'I knew that I was interested in the board position, I'd been gathering and accumulating knowledge. When I joined the Veblen Director Programme as an Apprentice it was really challenging for me at first because it was out of my own level of knowledge. I was part of a cohort, a small group of people going through this learning process, learning the new language and the new ideas. We went through it together, and it wasn't so scary eventually.'

Her Apprenticeship was a blend of observation and active learning. Marisa grappled with unfamiliar challenges, which pushed her to adapt and expand her knowledge base. The experience wasn't just about attending meetings; it involved in-depth engagement with board materials, contributing to discussions, and understanding the nuances of board dynamics. Marisa learnt the importance of balancing listening with contributing, realising that absorbing information was as crucial as sharing insights.

'It's good to have the exposure without too much of the responsibility. I think of it as a stepping stone and a really good chance to learn and to get exposure to what it's like to be in those kinds of meetings.'

One of Marisa's key realisations was the practical application of theoretical knowledge. She learnt that effective board participation goes beyond understanding concepts; it's about applying them strategically to impact decision-making. This insight was especially relevant in navigating the complexities of environmental, social, and governance (ESG) criteria in corporate settings.

Looking Forward: As her Apprenticeship neared its end, Marisa was pleased with her growth and the skills she had gained. She recognised the value of patience in observing organisational progress and the need for a longer-term perspective to see tangible results. Her experience reinforced her commitment to align with organisations that resonate with her values, especially in sustainability.

'I'd like to get another board position... even if I'm not doing anything it still requires reading, attending meetings, and communicating. These are all skills to continually improve.'

Marisa's journey on the board is a stepping stone to further opportunities. She now has a deeper understanding and a clearer vision of how she can contribute to sustainable corporate governance. She's ready to take on more significant roles in the future.

It's not about you; it's about the company

Hopefully the message is starting to sink in by now that you become a board director by adding value to the company.

There is no company out there that is currently thinking: 'You know what, the biggest problem we face right now is how we can help the reader of this book to get a nicely paid board seat. What can we do?!'

This may seem obvious to you that companies are not sitting around waiting to help you out, and yet I used to get dozens of messages from people on LinkedIn requesting board seats, and the pitches would often start 'I have 20 years of Operations experience, I think I could make a real difference to your board.' Well in one sense they were right, they would make a real difference to our board. All the other board members would be focused on long-term shareholder value and they would be focused on how they could improve operations 'in' the business. Not what a board is looking for.

To be fair, as I mentioned at the start of the book there is very little information about what goes on in boards, and so some people would guess and assume they could come into the boards basically as consultants to the company. It was completely wrong, but it was understandable.

The other type of pitch I used to get was no less common, but absolutely inexcusable to my mind.

'Hi, I see you're on the board of X company, I am coming to the end of my career and want to work less hours with less stress so would be willing to join your board.'

Well yes, that's exactly what I'm looking for! Someone lazier than me. How much can I pay you for such services?!

And this was not isolated. For a while I was getting requests like this every few weeks.

The point is that in both of these cases the individual did not understand, or did not care, what the company actually needed from the board, and so it didn't really matter how nice or smart or well-connected they were, or even how many boards they applied to. They would never get a look in because they were focused on themselves and what they wanted and not how to add value to the board.

Fortunately that is not you. You are now learning the problems and the pain points that companies face as they grow and how you can you can solve them. This is a good step on the way to becoming a Great Board Member.

Five components for great companies

Veblen Mantra #2
'Don't apply for board positions, create them'

In this section we learnt about some of the pressing problems that all companies, and especially PLCs, are facing and how you can use the Trojan Horse of the Apprentice Programme to help solve them and elevate your career to the big leagues (or at least the small companies in the big leagues).

1. Connections

I didn't want to tell you this earlier, because I didn't want you to become disheartened, but it's definitely harder to connect with great people as a 'wannabe' board member. However, now you are sitting on a board, even if it is an unpaid advisory role (nobody needs to know what, or if, you're getting paid), you have become infinitely more attractive to other board members, entrepreneurs and investors.

Leverage your new position to reach out to others and make new connections. Continue with connecting to directors and entrepreneurs but now is the time to really increase your investor network. The more connected you are to investors, the more valuable you will become to boards of all persuasions. Especially focus on ESG and Impact investors as they will be most interested in the work you're doing.

2. Knowledge

Get inquisitive. What can you learn about the industry? About the company? About the challenges and opportunities facing your executives today? At this stage you really want to be learning about Investor Relations (see next section) and all things related to ESG and the capital markets.

The people that I have learnt the most from over the years are often the ones that say the least but ask the smartest questions. I remember as a very young and wet behind the ears entrepreneur pitching two very successful business owners my current product (SMS based mobile services). Both of them politely heard me out and then asked me a variation of this question: 'Where is the multimillion dollar opportunity in this industry?'

Whether they asked me that question because they were trying to help me expand my horizons, or whether it was because they genuinely wanted to know the answer for their own means, over time it slowly dawned on me that I didn't really know the answer, but that it was a very important question.

And the inverse of this is that now you are a board Advisor or Apprentice, you may feel the need to contribute. But are you really qualified to do so, or is it just your ego that wants you to say something?

This is why the Apprentice Programme is so powerful. You get to build incredible knowledge around investors and ESG reporting that, even if the current company can't make you an offer at the end of the year, you know will be hugely valuable to other companies in the same situation.

3. Profile

What sounds better 'Aspiring Board Member' or 'Board Member'?

The answer is obvious. As soon as you get that role, make sure you update your LinkedIn profile, add it to your bio and add it to your email signatures.

Whilst you might know an Advisory position is nothing more than meeting a start-up founder for coffee and a chat once a month and an Apprentice Board Member is mostly sitting quietly and observing, nobody else knows or needs to know that.

Sitting on a PLC board, even as an Apprentice, is a whole new level of credibility.

We're also at the time to start being a bit more proactive about our profile. Time to move beyond LinkedIn.

For example, can you get interviewed on a podcast? When it comes to media, most of us have this idea that getting media coverage means getting into the publications that we read. A mention in *The FT* for example, or a simple cover of *Forbes* maybe?

The reality is that we have not done anything near remarkable enough to attract that attention, and that is fine. We don't need it. Start at the bottom of the media ladder and follow the philosophy of this book by adding value.

I like podcasts for this reason There are a million podcasts out there and new ones starting every day. That means that there are always podcast hosts out there looking for guests. Not the Tim Ferris and Joe Rogans of the world but people like yourself who start a podcast to meet some interesting people and build their profile, and then discover that if you don't have any audience no one wants to talk to you and if you can't get big names on your podcast then you can't attract an audience.

It's a cruel world, but again their problem presents your opportunity. You can reach out to those podcast hosts and promise that if interviewed about your career and board journey, you will share their podcast with your audience. (You don't need to mention that your audience is currently limited to your mum and your best friend!)

The point is not that this podcast is going to make you famous, the point is the first few podcasts you do are all about learning how to answer questions in the media. They also become the stepping stone you can use to get on more podcasts. And from there to bigger podcasts.

Finally, it's worth looking at the 'Board Recommendable' quiz in the Board Pack. You should be starting to reach a stage now where your opportunities will come from people recommending you to other people. Part of the reason that people are wary of recommending you is they don't want to risk looking bad if you mess up. This is why it is so important for you to get that first Board Advisory role and then let your network know about it. This alone makes it easier for them to recommend you, because someone else has already vouched for you by giving you a seat.

4. Value

It's really time to become a student of value. A big part of that is going to be understanding the relationship between investors and companies. If you are able to introduce the right investors to the right companies you can literally transform the trajectory of the business. You can also potentially cut yourself into deals and start making some real money along the way.

Hopefully you are also starting to understand that in this whole section about the problems boards face and the solutions you can provide to them I never once mentioned any skills, experience or qualifications you needed. If you can solve a big enough problem, none of those things are important. Don't let it be an excuse in your mind.

If you are the person on the board that can coordinate and produce an ESG report for investors, or if you are the person that can introduce and enable ESG funds to invest in the PLC, you become exceptionally valuable.

5. Leverage

People tend to get intimidated by PLCs. I'm not going to sugar-coat it. There is a lot more money involved, typically a lot more staff with mortgages to pay, a lot more investors and a lot more scrutiny, but potentially a lot more reward.

Also, if you are serious about a board career sooner or later you are going to need to bite the PLC bullet. I would encourage sooner rather than later.

Hopefully this section has shown you that basically the premise is the same as an Advisory Board, and that if you are genuinely enthusiastic to help and provide value, you can solve a real problem for PLCs.

Of course the goal is not to remain an Apprentice for long. A year is probably enough. Once you know you are delivering huge value it is time to mention wanting to move to an actual NED position so you can increase your level of contribution.

The beauty of an Apprentice programme is that expectations of you are low, your value creation is high and, if that company doesn't want to make you permanent, they are going to struggle to replace you. Other companies will leap at the chance to bring you on board with your demonstrable track record.

Those ESG investors you've brought in might also want to start talking to you about their other investments.

---

1. Investopedia, http://www.investopedia.com/ , the world's leading source of financial content on the web.

2. Patton, A, *Men, Money, and Motivation: Executive Compensation as an Instrument of Leadership*, republished by Literary Licensing in 2012

PART 3

Great Investors

I want to be a board member; why do I need to know about investors?

The truth is, you can actually sit on any board in the world – if you have enough money. Want to sit on Tesla's board? Go into the market and start buying. Apple? Call your broker. Once you have a big enough percentage of their stock you start to control votes and that gives you options. Including voting for yourself to be on the board.

It's no different in the small companies we've been looking at. In fact it's considerably easier. They're looking for investors. You will invest, but in return you want a seat on the board. Job done.

However, I'm assuming if you have got this far into the book, you are not looking to buy your way on to a board. Yet.

But here is why this is still relevant. If anyone can get on the board with the right investment capital, then that means if you are 'connected' to capital you also have a much higher chance of getting a board seat as the board will want to use you to get to the investment.

In fact this idea is so powerful, that finding the right investor is like finding Willy Wonka's Golden Ticket.

The biggest and the brightest investors don't want to sit on boards themselves. They don't have the time, and whilst companies would love to have the cachet and experience they could provide, it is much more likely that the investor will send in one of their minions to sit on the board and oversee their investments. Want to be a well-paid minion?

What this means for you is that when you join a board, you should make it a point to try and meet with your investors. If you can turn that investor into an ally, usually by helping them to get the best returns for their investment or at the very least being available and clear with your communication, then there is a strong chance they will want you to help them on other boards they have investments in.

Uncover the investor mindset to reach the pot of gold

The first board you join as an Advisor is likely to be a small private company or start-up. In this case you may only have one shareholder, the business owner. However, as we discussed in the Great Companies section, not every business owner is actually thinking in terms of what is best for themselves as a shareholder. That is part of the value that you bring, to help them focus on shareholder value. In fact one exceptionally useful piece of advice you can give them is for them to start an Advisory Board for someone else's company.

Most entrepreneurs are so focused on their own problems that they can get massive value by seeing how other companies operate, and ultimately both companies will benefit. Perhaps there could even be a useful book you could suggest they read...

The next step up from one shareholder is a handful of shareholders.

Tech start-ups often fall into this category. An unfortunate consequence of some of the brilliance we have seen come out of Silicon Valley over the past few decades is that most new entrepreneurs now believe the way you grow a business is coming up with an idea and then raising money from investors.

Call me old school, but I'm still much more of a fan of coming up with an idea and selling it to clients. With a proven cash generating business model the investors often come to you which is a much better negotiating position to be in.

Anyway, for now there are still a multitude of companies that have more investors than clients. You may well find yourself on the board of such a company and it is important that you get a firm grasp on the ambitions of each investor.

The relationship between investor and CEO often starts off lovely and supportive in the beginning, but very soon where money is involved, things can quickly spiral in the wrong direction.

A more likely scenario you will come across is where investors are running out of, or have run out of, patience with a CEO who keeps promising great things in the future but is not actually delivering.

Even though it might have been the CEO that brought you on to the board, a big part of your responsibility is to all shareholders of the company, not just the person that gave you the job.

As we will discuss later, if you do a good job of representing an investor's interests on the board, you may find they become a perfect conduit to getting you more board seats to support their other investments.

But we're not there yet.

Think like an investor

When you are introducing yourself to investors and trying to represent their best interests, it is very difficult to have true empathy with their situation unless you understand what it is like to have invested in a company. This disconnect is often what causes a breakdown between CEOs and shareholders.

Founders, who tend to not be that wealthy themselves because all their money goes back into growing their business, are often completely unaware of what it feels like to risk your own money on someone else. Of course as a founder you are risking all your own money on your staff etc., but at least you have control, or at least the illusion of control, over how it is spent.

Consequently founders can find it hard to empathise with investors.

It's not just founders. Sadly, many board members, especially executive directors, have zero empathy for investors because they themselves have never been investors.

- They don't understand why investors invest.

- They don't understand their motivations, their concerns.

Oftentimes this lack of understanding comes across as a lack of interest which can further antagonise the situation. Remember the CEOs who wasted our time with product demos instead of investor presentations?

My view is that if you are going to be a board member you should be an investor too. I believe you should have made at least one private investment and several public investments. Not for the financial return, but for learning.

In the Veblen programme, one of the first exercises we have our members do is to try to buy $100 worth of a micro-cap company on the public markets, and then try to explain their decision, and challenges, to their accountability board. The problem they quickly come across is that most micro-caps do a truly horrible job of helping educate investors on why they should invest. And even when everything is good, finding a broker that will actually let you buy micro-cap stocks can be a challenge. Especially if the company is overseas.

One of the biggest takeaways from this section is to start thinking about your investors not as investors but as clients. And stock in your company as the product you are selling. This is important for fundraising for small companies, but incredibly important when you get into the public markets, and will automatically put you ahead of 99% of the companies out there.

The other advice we give our clients is to start looking at angel investing. NOT, and I want to emphasise this, as a good investment choice (you have better odds of hitting the jackpot by playing the lottery), but as a great way to start understanding about business and building relationships with founders.

Becoming an angel investor, even if it s one small investment, can be worth it in terms of the lessons you learn. It is also another board you can potentially add yourself to.

Personally I don't do any angel or early-stage investing. To me the maths don't stack up as an investment option, but they absolutely stack up if you are trying to learn about business, entrepreneurship and investing.

Learning to invest / Investing to learn

As a young entrepreneur I always assumed that at some point in the future I would 'make it' and be worth millions. Making it was the most important thing and was what drove to me to get up each day. The actual 'millions' side of things didn't really interest me that much. Yes I wanted the lifestyle it could afford, but I didn't actually have much of an interest in money itself. I assumed that once I had enough I would hire some wealth advisor in a sharp suit who would take care of all that stuff, and just ensure there was always enough in the bank for the school fees and the nice holidays and that through clever investments my nest egg would keep growing.

Turns out this is an incredibly expensive and unhelpful mindset.

Investing is such a vast and complex field it is no wonder people are put off trying to understand it. In fact the entire industry is pretty much designed to confuse you so much that you decide not to think for yourself and just 'trust' someone else with your money.

But sadly, this is not thinking like an owner.

It has become cool to say 'I'm not interested in money'. And for good reason as a society we ostracise those who are obsessed with it, but part of being a grown-up is understanding how to turn your money into more money and taking responsibility for your decisions in this area.

So let's first separate Learning to Invest and Investing to Learn.

Step 1. Start investing

Whilst you've been reading this book, I have been psychoanalysing you, checking your spending habits, your risk profile, your peers, your family, your aspirations, your probable date of retirement and your expected death date. Firstly, congratulations on all you have achieved to date, and what a long and exciting life you have ahead of you – I'm impressed and slightly jealous!

Secondly, based on all the data I have collected on you, I can tell you that the best investment for the bulk of your funds is...

A low fee ETF (Exchange Traded Fund). How do I know this? Because consistently, over the long term it will give you the best results. For now, just trust me on that. Anyone else that offers to manage your money for you is going to take a fee for doing so and that is not in your best interests.

Step 2. Start learning

The great thing about an ETF is that you can 'set and forget' – stick a portion of your salary in each month, don't look at it, and it will automatically compound. In the short term it won't appear very exciting; over the long term it will outperform every 'new and exciting' investment hype that the masses are screaming about (AI, Crypto, Web 2.0, Real Estate, eCommerce, .Com, Oil, Tulips etc.).

The disadvantage is that you are not going to learn anything about investing from watching your ETF. If you do choose to watch it every day, it's like watching paint dry but constantly second-guessing yourself as to whether it was the right paint colour in the first place. I strongly recommend against it.

To actually start learning, you need some 'learning' capital. Yes, you could 'pretend' invest, but part of why we are learning to invest is that the biggest stakeholders you will be dealing with when you sit on the board are shareholders. Shareholders are likely to get quite emotional about their investments. It is impossible for you to empathise with an investor unless you too have felt some of the pain and/or elation that comes with an investing decision.

> Investing vs Trading: This is too big a discussion to get into here, but our job is not to trade shares. Trading is dependent on market timing and the smartest people in the world with all the analysts and computing power available cannot get it right consistently (despite what YouTubers with pretty charts will show you). If you want to trade for fun, all power to you, but don't confuse it with investing which is focused on long-term returns.

Your personal wealth

You shouldn't need to be wealthy to be an effective board member, but equally it is hard to be truly focused on making decisions that are worth millions, or billions, to the company if you don't have your own house in order. Personal wealth is too big a topic for this book, but as it relates to boards I would say three things.

Firstly, if it's not already, get your house in order.

A lot of people get carried away with thinking about earning millions when they don't actually know how to earn an extra $1k per month. This is a valuable skill for you personally to have because you will likely find yourself having the same conversation with a small business owner at some point in the future. Obsessed with winning the big ticket, but unable to focus on what they can do today to add another $1k to the bottom line.

Whilst you don't need to be wealthy, nobody wants to be advised by someone who can't manage their own finances. That means, if you are currently in a fragile place financially, or mentally, that is something you need to fix for yourself before you start trying to help others. Again, you don't need to be wealthy, but you don't want to be struggling either.

Secondly, keep your eyes open

Dr Keith Kantor knew when he started advising companies that by making one or two introductions he could completely change the trajectory of a company's growth path. He also knew the value of doing that and so negotiated with the companies. If I can help you achieve X (where X is a revenue target or market cap, or profit margins) would that be worth Y to you (cash bonus, monthly salary, a slice of equity)?

He was able to negotiate for himself some very lucrative deals because for the founders who agreed to them it was all upside, and for Keith he was confident in his ability to deliver.

You may not have the experience and connections that Keith had to be able to do this on day one, but the more you play this game, the more opportunities you will see to cut yourself a slice of the action. Keep looking beyond what's right in front of you.

Thirdly, nobody needs to know you' financial situation

Let me share something that I've noticed from some of the wealthiest people I've ever met. They are often short of cash. Mostly they have the cash tied up in other return generating assets, and whilst they might want what it is they are buying, they don't have the funds handy to do so. Hence they might agree to buy a car, a house, a company, and yet when it comes time to close the deal and receive the funds they have a habit of dragging their feet. Sometimes it's purposeful; other times they are just in a long chain of people where they are waiting for someone to give them their funds for some assets. Other times they are just dragging their heels knowing that the price will eventually come down or something better might come up.

What you never hear a wealthy person say is 'I can't afford it'.

Then you look at the average person, and, when presented with an opportunity, you will often hear 'I can't afford it'. Because right then and there at that time they do not have the cash available. What is the difference? In both cases the individual didn't have cash available, but in the first case they will continue to receive opportunities. In the second instance the opportunities will not waste their time with this individual in the future.

When you join a board, the nature of the society we live in is that people will think that you have 'made it' at least in one regard. The assumption will be, often wrongly, that you are making lots of money as a board member. There is nothing wrong with letting people make this assumption about you and it will certainly lead to more opportunities coming your way.

However, you can very easily destroy this illusion with the words you use. Saying you can't afford something, talking about how uncomfortable the bus or flying economy is, or complaining about the price of something is a great way to advertise to the world that you are not there yet financially. You don't need to buy things you can't afford. Some of the wealthiest people I know spend nothing on fancy cars or clothes, but they also make sure the right people know they have access to funds if needed and they are open to opportunities, even if they don't have the cash today.

Rightly or wrongly the world trusts those that are perceived as successful. This creates opportunities which in turn allow you to become successful.

Try banishing the words 'I can't afford it' from your lips. When someone offers you an opportunity to buy something, to invest, to travel somewhere, think about what you would say if you could easily afford it but don't currently have the cash because it's tied up in investments?

I am not advocating lying or misleading someone about your wealth; that is fraud and not the point at all. The point is that no one has any right to know what your personal wealth is and that once you achieve a high level of personal wealth it does not mean you have unlimited cash flow. When you do make it, you will certainly have lots of options how to invest it.

Many people who chase wealth do so in the belief that once they have it they will not need to worry about it. They don't want to think about it. No one likes scrabbling around trying to find money for bills and constantly having to worry about the cost of things.

This belief is not only wrong it is actually detrimental to the accumulation of wealth. The wealthy actually spend much more time thinking about their money. Where is it? What return is it generating? What is the probability of losing it? Who is after it? How can I leverage it better?

Certainly I could have been considerably further along the wealth ladder now if I had begun asking those questions much earlier in my career.

Like any game the more we practice the better we get, but there are always enough variables that the game never gets easier. Luck, timing and human unpredictability can all conspire against us. Yet the more cycles we go through the more we can start to bend the odds in our favour.

As a board member, the more cycles you go through the better you will become and the better you will get at recognising patterns.

The reality is that getting on the right board and helping that company to succeed can create transformational levels of wealth for you and those around you. Despite the 50/50 odds, the public markets do still have the ability to create exponential gains.

And whilst I think that sitting on boards and getting involved in investing and deals is the best way to learn, it is often useful to understand the history so we have some context.

To understand the future, study the past we must

Europeans started trading debt (promissory notes or bonds as we more commonly call them today) back in the twelfth century or possibly even earlier. In Antwerp (Belgium), which was the centre of international trade, in the 1300s more formalised trading was created by the Venetians to trade government bonds. The Antwerp stock exchange began in 1531 but still mostly traded bonds.

At that stage most business was driven by ships' captains trying to raise money to go overseas and open trade routes, plunder for gold etc. Incidentally, a skipper of a boat comes from the Dutch word for Schipp which ultimately led to words we recognise today like entrepreneurship, leadership etc.

Meanwhile in Frankfurt, Germany people had been trading coins, silver and gold in what we would now consider a currency exchange since the eleventh century at mediaeval fairs. The most popular would ultimately evolve into what we know as the Frankfurt Stock Exchange, or Börse Frankfurt, that we know today. Somewhat ironically for a country with such a steeped history of trading, the conservative Germans today have the lowest share ownership per head of population of any developed country (Sweden has the highest).

Famously in Holland the first 'modern' stock exchange as we know it today was created to trade shares in the Dutch East India company in 1611. (OK, I concede it may only be famous to us business geeks!)

The Dutch also originated Wall St in New York some thirty years later (literally buying and selling stocks up against a wall). Although it was 200 years after that before the New York stock exchange as we know it was formalised.

Back in London, in the 1700s, in a coffee shop, they started posting prices of stocks on the wall, and in 1800 the London Stock Exchange was officially created to try to stomp out some of the many scams and fraudsters that were abusing this high tech coffee-based, note-pinning, communications system.

Two hundred years later the battle between scams and regulators still carries on.

But why all the interest in trading stocks? Everything comes down to funding and liquidity. Entrepreneurs want funding for their investments, whether that's to sail a ship to foreign lands or build an app to improve your shopping experience. Investors want returns, but they also want liquidity (i.e. the ability to trade that ownership of stock back for cash whenever they need it).

Fast forward to the modern markets of the last seventy plus years. The most efficient way for a business owner to raise capital was to do an IPO, an initial public offering. The public could buy a slice of that company, in effect a promissory note to get a share of all future profits. Typically new stock is created and the money goes into the company for growth. Over the centuries, more and more regulations have been created to stop the manipulation of markets and the exploitation of investors, but it is still a far from efficient system. The first insider trading rule was put in place in 1909, but it was definitely not clear or enforceable. Whilst US congress tried to tighten it up in 1934 it still did not actually define what constituted insider trading. There have been numerous high-profile cases, especially in the 1980s, but there still remains a lot of scope for improvement. Consequently investors often remain very wary of new listings and small businesses.

The price of stock multiplied by the number of shares on issue determines the market cap of the company and the 'value' of that company. And yet on a regular basis in the markets we see 'darlings' of the stock market shoot up hundreds of percentage points, and then lose 90% of their value in six months when arguably nothing material has changed within the company.

The dot-com boom was one example of this, but we also saw it with so-called 'Covid' stocks like Zoom or Peloton that became all the rage and then just as quickly fell out of favour with investors.

So the market cap is a product of the buyers and the sellers of shares on those days. And that is often determined by the narrative about 'equity story'. More demand for shares, price goes up; less demand (or more demand to swap those shares for cash) and price goes down. In the short term, the fundamentals of the business are *almost* irrelevant.

So how does all this relate to you as a board member?

Firstly, the IPOs you have probably heard of, the ones that get all the public attention like Facebook or Alibaba are completely different entities from 99% of the stock market, so there is not too much we can learn from them. They are also not likely to be the boards you start on.

We're going to focus on the other 99% of companies that are small or micro-cap as this is likely where you will begin your journey.

Let's start with the bad news: as mentioned previously, 50% of public companies list and their share price goes backwards. This bears repeating. One out of every two listings are net destroyers of shareholder value. They never go back to their initial listing price. In fact, in the last twenty years, of all 60,000 publicly listed companies 100% of shareholder returns were delivered by just 1,500 companies, which is just 2.3%.[1] (Think Apple, Microsoft, Amazon etc.)

Now, if you fancy yourself as a stock picker, and remember there is a multi-trillion dollar industry full of people that do, you can see how hard it is to pick winners. And bear in mind that over that twenty-year period, many of those top companies were underwater for a decade or more. Meaning if you owned Apple or Microsoft (considered great stocks at time of writing), you would have been underperforming the broader market for more than a decade after the dot-com bubble burst. That is a very long time to be underwater and maintain your confidence in the stock

So from a board perspective there is a pretty strong chance that you will be on the board of a company with investors that have lost money by investing with your company. That is important to know as the dynamic of investor relations shifts significantly when returns are good vs the alternative.

Since we're covering history, let's just segue into Exchange Traded Funds (ETFs) as they are an important player in this game.

Basically owning a selection or an 'index' of the companies on a particular exchange. The idea being that overall markets go up, so, rather than try to pick winners, hold a percentage of all and reap the rewards.

John Bogle created Vanguard in the 1970s to do just that. And it was a complete failure. For nearly a decade it did nothing. No investors wanted 'average' they wanted above average. Even though almost all stock pickers underperform the market over any length of time, it wasn't in anyone's interests to admit that.

It's the reason why Warren Buffett CEO of Berkshire Hathaway and one of richest men on the planet is so famous; he is a rarity in the field by being consistently above average.

Now, ETFs have typically averaged 10–11% per year over the past forty years.[2] Not too dusty. So if you're sensible you don't try to time the market, you don't try to bet on individual stocks, and you just invest in tracker funds.

Those funds keep going up, even as individual stocks drop out of them and new ones enter. Which is why I recommended them for the bulk of your investment capital.

Supply and Demand

Back to IPOs. This used to be pretty much the only way to get investment capital for companies. But a 50% failure rate is not very appealing, so why does it have such a high failure rate?

It all comes down to liquidity and specifically demand for the stock. You see when companies list, not only do they create more stock for new investors, often existing investors want to get their own liquidity. For founders and staff this is a chance to 'take some chips off the table'. Early investors want to cash in their returns so they can reinvest that capital in other projects. Even the investment banks that take the companies public often take stakes in the company beforehand with a view to selling as much as they can for as big a profit as possible on listing.

The net result is that when a company lists there are an awful lot of people trying to sell their stock for cash.

If there are more sellers than buyers, then the share price goes down. When investors look at a stock, if the share price is going down, they decide not to buy. Those people still holding the stock start to panic and decide to sell before it gets any lower, which leads to a downward 'death' spiral.

Some exchanges have minimum company values which a company must adhere to which means if they drop below that they will be delisted.

There is a saying in investing: 'The trend is your friend – until the end.'

Despite what people will tell you about fundamental investing, or wanting to understand the management or the macro environment or the investing 'moat' or any of these other indications of sophistication, the majority of investors will only invest in stocks going up and they will exit stocks that are going down. The market tends to move as a herd.

Bitcoin proves this. There are no 'business fundamentals'. It is valuable because we all agree it is valuable. We buy when more people agree, and we sell when fewer people agree. We might comfort ourselves with a narrative about it being 'anti-establishment' or 'digital gold', but basically we are following a chart.

Where does this leave you as a board member?

It is most likely that one or more of the small cap boards you are going to be sitting on are going to be underwater (below the original share price), and wanting to try to figure out how to increase shareholder returns.

In most cases, because they are not experts in the stock market, but are experts in their industry, they will return to what they know: try to add more customers, cut more costs, make more profit and hope the share price goes up.

That is not unimportant but it's not the whole story either. Remember that there have been plenty of companies in the last couple of decades that list and their share price goes up even if they are not making profit. And there have been plenty of profitable companies that have fallen out of favour and the share price has plummeted.

The most valuable thing you can do to help in this case is package the story and manage investor relations. For those that really want to understand how you can 'solve' the negative share price issue, I have included a video on 'Constrained Stock Model' in the Board Pack at

Investor Relations

Small companies to big companies.

One of the biggest areas of value you can offer to a board is to focus on Investor Relations. For most companies this doesn't need to be more complicated than speaking to, and more importantly, listening to your shareholders. Social media offers an unprecedented view of what your shareholders actually think.

Time for an important caveat here. When I discussed how valuable it is to interact with investors and to build a personal profile, I found that most traditional board members were dead set against it. The reason was more often than not fear based on ignorance. Some of it was founded, some of it not.

There are plenty of ways you can fall foul of securities laws as soon as you start talking about a public company. In a bid to avoid this, many directors decide the simplest option is to say nothing.

This is a cop-out, and in my opinion more of an excuse not to have to 'deal with' investors than a genuine attempt to avoid regulation.

Whilst I'm definitely not a securities lawyer, the list of things you can't talk about is not actually that daunting.

The basic thing that securities law in most countries is concerned about is that 'material' information gets passed to all shareholders at the same time through official channels. This is to stop the dissemination of insider information and insider trading. It therefore has to go out on a pre-formatted press release through a very expensive distribution channel and normally has to be approved by dozens of people before it goes out. What you can't do is call up a friend or go on social media and say 'here are our annual results' before it has gone through this process.

So what can you say? Well first off let's look at 'material'. Generally speaking this is anything that is deemed important enough that it might impact somebody's ownership decision.

Firing your janitor, not material.

Winning a new contract that is more than 5% of your annual turnover, material.

Hiring a senior manager is material; launching a new marketing campaign, probably not material.

You certainly should not talk about the price of your stock and you definitely cannot make any forecasts in public.

This is where entrepreneurs tend to get themselves in trouble. As a private company, talking about how great business is is the default communications standard, so it can come as a shock to have to rein it in when you go public.

I found many directors use this fear of saying something wrong to not engage at all. Whilst I think this is wrong-headed, it creates a huge opportunity for you as the new board member. If you are the person at the board table who is happy to talk to, and more importantly listen to, investors and then provide to the board genuine insights into what they are thinking, that is hugely valuable.

As well as social media, each country has a series of investor forums that can be gold for information on what investors are thinking. Again, some words of caution, internet forums are weird places with some weird people. You need a thick skin to go in there as they will hold no punches if they think you are doing a bad job. However, in the past with companies whose boards I have sat on, by reading what our investors were posting, we were able to make several changes to the way we reported information to make sure that things which were obvious to us were being more clearly communicated to others.

It is human nature to get defensive when someone is trashing you and your company in the forums or on social media, but absolutely do not engage. You're not Elon Musk; you don't need to troll people for fun. Bite your tongue, focus on what you can learn and rise above it.

Because most board members of small cap stocks are likely to be exec directors and pretty focused on the day-to-day running of their business they can be quite dismissive of investors because they don't really understand them.

By talking to your investors, big and small, you can learn valuable data that can shape the way you decide strategy at board level.

Hiring a board member on merit

I've touched on this earlier, but now we're looking at it from the investor's perspective it deserves looking at again.

And it deserves looking at again because what I'm arguing is counter-intuitive and provokes the most criticism – but bear with me.

Right now you want a board seat. But to understand what a board is looking for, you need to be thinking like they would. You need to think like a board that is considering a new board member.

I think we can all agree that we should want the best, most experienced, most qualified person on the board. But apart from the obvious fact that 'best' is subjective, just because someone was the best on another board doesn't mean that in this company, this culture, this stage of the corporate journey, they will still be the best.

Let's take Warren Buffett. There are not many people out there with his knowledge, experience and connections. Theoretically, if you could afford him, he would likely be the best board member ever. The Michael Jordan of Boardrooms!

Unless... you're in a fast growth tech company for example. Warren is famously not a huge fan of tech. As a fast growth tech start-up you need to make some quick decisions and make some 'bet the company' moves.

No offence to the Sage of Omaha, but we're really not appealing to his strengths here. And just because he's one of the wealthiest men in the world does not mean he will invest in your company. In fact, I'm quite certain he would not.

So it's quite possible, he is not actually the 'best' board member for your company.

Now, let's say even though Warren is less than ideal in this context you still want him on the board, and because this is make-believe time, he begrudgingly agrees. But you still need funding.

You reach out to a well-known tech investor who likes your space and after a few discussions this investor decides they will invest. In fact they love your business. Not only will they invest the full $10m you're raising now, they are willing to invest $100m in the future to see you really maximise your potential. What a win! Ain't make-believe time fun?!

But they will, of course, need a board seat; after all they want to oversee and protect their investment. You're not going to pass up this opportunity, so you readily agree. The money goes into the bank, you begin scaling up the company and the date of the next board meeting quickly comes round.

As you walk into the room, you see Warren Buffett reading the prospectus of a company a thousand times bigger than yours and wondering to himself why he's here, and next to him you see a 10-year-old girl playing Roblox on an iPad.

Before you can ask, your CFO (Chief Financial Officer) informs you that the 10-year-old girl is the board representative, and the daughter, of your main tech investor.

In this scenario, who is the 'best' board member? Who is the most valuable to you? Warren's very successful playbook for success will not work in your start-up environment. And whilst the 10-year-old might not share many insights at a board meeting, your future access to funds is solely dependent on her being on the board and remaining happy.

This may seem like a crazy example, but it illustrates a very important point that you need to keep in mind. The most valuable thing you as a board member can provide to a business is almost always capital, or access to capital.

Even if companies don't need investment it gives them options, and options are everything. If you're still tied to the idea that board members should have twenty years of experience, a director's certificate and have written a thesis on good corporate governance, then you're missing the biggest point. You can be valuable to a board if you can help them unlock access to capital. For some boards that might be adding a 10-year-old girl.

And here we come back to diversity. For other companies it's adding a disabled person, an LGBTQ+ person, a foreigner, a young person or even an old white man, because that is what allows them to access new streams of investment from ESG funds.

The individual's talents are far less important than what the individual represents.

For the past 100+ years investors have been demanding that boards have 'experience' i.e. your typical grey-haired man who has sat on boards for the past twenty years. Companies had to add these people to the board to get access to the capital they needed. It had nothing to do with the individual's talents or contribution and everything to do with what the individual represented. Were they hired on merit?

More and more investment funds have mandates that mean they are no longer able to invest in companies that don't have diverse boards. That means that the most valuable person on the board is not the one with the MBA, the director's certificate and all the technical knowledge, it is the person that allows them to access the ESG fund.

And that could be you. Today.

Being a 'token' board member.

Does it matter? That's for you to decide. Remember we're not looking for your dream board job; we're looking to get your first paying board seat. It's not the final destination, it's just a stepping stone. And if it happens to be well-paid, high status and gets you much needed experience, does it actually matter if they are not really interested in your contribution and opinions?

You're on the bottom of the ladder and the only way is up!

I have lived in Asia for more than twenty years and as a Caucasian male I am very much a minority. For an Asian board trying to demonstrate to investors that they are serious about diversity, hiring me might be a useful step. Being a 'token' representative on their board might not be an ideal board position for me but if I was at the beginning of my board career it is one I would have leapt at.

As you can see, diversity on boards is not a Western problem. This topic comes up all over the world as investors recognise they want fresh thinking on boards. Which brings us back to the idea of thinking internationally. Everyone is diverse somewhere. Use that to your advantage.

It's a small world after all and the last step is never what you expect

This might be the biggest shift in thinking for you, but it's an important one. There are around 330 million companies in the world that could potentially benefit from you being on their board.[3] I've just checked on Google Maps and it turns out the vast majority of those companies are not in your local neighbourhood. They're not even in your country.

Whilst numbers are tricky to come by, the country with the most companies is the US, but that accounts for less than 10% of all companies worldwide.

Just basic law of averages should mean that it makes more sense to widen your search, but there are better reasons beyond that.

Let's say you're a 40-something manager in a company. You're ambitious, you want to get ahead, you like the idea of a board seat, but you know the chances to progress up the ladder in your current company are limited, and certainly no one on the board knows you exist, let alone wants to offer you a role.

So you start looking for board seats on companies. You don't want to leave the day job, so you start applying for board seats in your city, or a city near you.

We've already covered why applying for board seats is a bad idea, but even if it was a real opportunity you were apply ng for, and even if they did consider you, and even if they didn't care about your lack of experience and all those other things, you would still be wholly unremarkable, because pretty much everyone else who was applying would also be from the same city/country.

Now let's say you start applying for international boards (again we're not going to do this, I'm making a point!). Now your application stands out; you're from overseas. You have different experiences, different connections than everyone else who is applying locally. You are, believe it or not, 'exotic' (I always knew this about you, but not everyone recognises it). This makes you stand out. Especially if this company is looking to expand overseas.

But you have a job, family, responsibilities; you can't drop everything and travel the world to serve on a board!

Fortunately, due to Covid, it is not unusual for board meetings to happen 100% over Zoom. I regularly sit on boards where I have never even met the other board members. It truly is a small world after all...

What's important to note is that this conversation about diversity is happening everywhere I go in the world. I regularly talk to the entrepreneurial and inspiring early-stage businesses across Africa that are hungry for international experience to learn from and help them expand overseas. I have an office in the Middle East which probably more than any other region has capital to invest, but is equally constrained by not being able to invest in their own non-diverse boards. And here in Asia, if we look at countries like Japan, which have traditionally prided themselves on not having foreigners on boards, but have recently changed laws to make sure companies have at least two NEDs on their biggest companies.

A big part of this whole idea is to understand that other people can see value in us that we can't see. Don't underestimate how valuable your background and your geography might already be to the right company.

Deeper dive: Vikki Sylvester – Navigating the boardroom labyrinth

Initial foray into board governance: Vikki Sylvester's professional path began in social care, a journey that later led her to the educational sector and eventually to co-founding a successful family-owned training company. Despite her achievements, Vikki entered the world of board governance with little to no prior experience. Her initial venture into board roles marked the beginning of a significant transformation in her professional outlook.

Embracing voluntary board roles for growth: Vikki engaged in various voluntary board roles from 2007 to gain diverse experiences and develop new skills including becoming the chair of governors at a local school, independent governor at a university, and vice chair of an education organisation. These roles provided her with a different perspective from running her own business, teaching her the importance of facilitation and collaboration in a board setting. Through these experiences, Vikki learnt the value of being a minority voice in the room, bringing unique insights to the table. These roles were crucial in her transition from operational leader to strategic board member, helping her understand and adapt to the dynamics of board governance.

'Understanding boards meant nothing to me when I started our business. I had absolutely zero experience. My voluntary roles came about because I was convinced there had to be a better way of doing things. If you think something could be done better then step up and make a difference. Voluntary roles were really important because they gave me a different experience from being in my own business. In a voluntary role... you learn that you are not the driver, you're a facilitator.'

This move was strategic, allowing her to immerse herself in diverse governance cultures.

Developing strategic acumen: As Vikki's involvement in board roles deepened, so did her understanding of the intricacies of governance. She recognised the importance of bringing a unique perspective to the table, often being the minority voice in discussions.

'Being in a room with unfamiliar people, especially where the dynamics are constantly changing, can initially feel uncomfortable. I realised this discomfort was a learning opportunity and a chance to contribute uniquely. Now, I try to be the minority in a room... it means I'm bringing something that nobody else in the room can bring.'

This ability to offer fresh insights was not just beneficial for her personal growth but also for the organisations she served. Her approach to governance was marked by a commitment to ethical practices and a keen awareness of the evolving business landscape.

Championing good governance and diversity: Vikki's journey in the boardroom became synonymous with strong, ethical governance. She leveraged her position to advocate for diversity and inclusivity in decision-making processes. Her experiences underscored the need for board members to be adaptable, forward-thinking and open to learning from every situation.

'The real benefit of ESG lies in its holistic impact. It's not just about looking good on paper; it's about genuinely creating a positive ripple effect. When you commit to the right practices, you naturally attract more customers and foster a more committed workforce. It's about building a proactive, positive culture, where everyone feels they're contributing to something meaningful. The pandemic and global challenges have shifted investor attitudes significantly towards ESG. There's a growing realisation that investments should not only yield financial returns but also contribute positively to society and the environment.'

If a company is doing the right things, it is more likely to attract customers and employees. As a board member you can influence the ESG policy.

Impactful leadership and future aspirations: Today, Vikki stands as a testament to the transformative power of strategic board involvement. Her focus has consistently been on driving positive changes within organisations, emphasising the role of board members in shaping future business trajectories. Vikki continues to champion the need for ongoing personal and professional development, recognising that the challenges of modern governance require continuous learning and adaptation.

Hiring winners and losers

A further note on hiring as it is so critical to the companies you advise, and also why the Apprentice programme is so effective.

When I was a young entrepreneur I had a mentor of sorts who ran a very successful below the line marketing agency. I was a struggling entrepreneur and I had just made a very expensive hire that turned out to be a complete disaster. I remember asking my mentor who had about 500 staff how to recruit good people and she shared with me her story.

When she first started out, she would hire on instinct. Normally within the first few minutes of an interview she had made up her mind; the rest of the conversation was just a waste of time. In this way she had found some incredible people. People that had joined her at the lowest positions in her organisation, been loyal and hard-working, and were still with her and in her senior management team today. However, it wasn't particularly consistent and at least half of the people she had hired didn't work out.

As the company grew, hiring people that didn't work out became more and more costly, and she decided that she needed to learn about recruitment. She learnt that best practice was to have multiple people involved in the hiring decision and to compile a list of good questions that really got to the heart of what people had done and achieved in the past. This process took a lot longer, but felt a lot more 'professional', made her existing employees feel like they had more of a say and made a lot of sense.

But the results were not great. After a couple of years when they analysed who had worked out and who had failed, they discovered that it was about the same ratio as before, but the extra time taken was costing the business.

Her next evolution was reading a book that told her that actually, whatever your interview process is, the biggest determinant of whether an employee will work out or not is your onboarding process. Starbucks and McDonalds were great examples of this. All over the world spotty teenagers say the same things and serve you the same way due to the training they receive. Up until that point, like most busy entrepreneurs, her onboarding was pretty non-existent. She just expected people to hit the ground running, but now she realised that without a decent onboarding process she was setting up her employees for failure.

She brought in the heads of all her departments. They got rid of weeks of interviews, and instead they built a kick-ass three-month onboarding process for all new hires. This would help them find their way around this dynamic organisation, would train them in the values of the company, exactly what was expected of them and how they could thrive in this environment. Everyone agreed they wished that they had had this when they joined.

However, after a couple of high profile hiring disasters, they did yet another analysis and discovered – yeah, it had made no difference.

Everyone felt like it should work better but actually some people turned out to be winners and others turned out to be completely out of their depth.

As I sat and listened to this story, what she was saying all made perfect sense, but I was keen for her to get the 'secret' I could learn from her.

She leaned forward and said, 'Basically it's all rubbish. Some people work out, some people don't. It's impossible to know who will, so write bad hires off as the cost of doing business.'

Not really what I wanted to hear and know that there will be people reading this outraged and claiming that they have a perfect hiring record. It's something I have mulled over a lot during the hundreds of people I have hired over the years.

I realised I too had a perfect hiring record when I worked at UUnet WorldCom, the number one internet service provider in the world at the height of the dot com boom. As a young network operations manager of an incredibly fast-growing company I had to hire lots of people. And I did. And they were great.

But it turns out there is a huge difference in hiring people when you work at one of the most attractive companies in the world to work for and have basically unlimited resources. Plus by the time I actually got to interview candidates they had been vetted by the recruitment company, then our internal HR team and then they ended up at my desk. And I hired based on whether they would be fun to work with on night shift. And they were.

Looking back quite a few of them were basically useless, but we were growing so fast and needed bodies so I think at that point it would have been nearly impossible to be fired. In fact I made some pretty epic and costly mistakes in my job and kept getting promoted, so that kinda proves the point.

Yes I had a 100% hiring success rate. But if I'm honest, anyone could have that. The type of people attracted to joining a big corporation with all the associated perks are very different from those joining a start-up or a small cap company with a struggling share price.

Sadly you don't get to hire the people you want to hire. You hire the people you can afford. And typically those are the people that don't have too many other options. Amazingly, oftentimes these people turn out to be complete stars and can grow in the business with you, but again you have to admit that's more by luck than by design.

Fortunately as I was building my entrepreneurial chops, needing to hire more and more people across my businesses, the internet was starting to enable a wave of freelancing. I decided that I wanted to exploit the opportunities to hire incredible people on cheaper hourly rates and see what I could achieve.

Like for most people who try this, it was a disaster to start with. I went for the cheapest people and often ended up spending a fortune to find out they couldn't do the job (or often that I just hadn't given them a good enough brief). Over time I got better at breaking down tasks and paying for results, but the best improvement came when I allocated a small bit of my budget to testing at least three freelancers for each project. Fifty to a hundred dollars for them each to do a quick mini project. I quickly discovered which ones could follow instructions, who communicated well and who delivered on time.

The freelancers that worked well with me I would end up giving more and more work to. And on more than one occasion I ended up giving them so much work they ended up running my companies.

I don't think I have hired anyone 'full-time' as a normal hire for at least five years now. Everyone I hire now starts off as a freelancer and then as long as they deliver I keep adding responsibilities.

The problem with traditional hiring, as my mentor had found out, is that past behaviour is no real predictor of future behaviour. Now I'm not saying that good interview practice, onboarding, reference checking etc. are a complete waste of time; they're clearly not. However, just because someone has worked well in a certain culture and environment in the past does not mean that they are going to work well for you in the future.

The fact is we just don't know. Maybe they won't get on with a key member of staff. Maybe they will have some crisis in their home life that wasn't on the table before. Maybe they have an existential crisis. Who knows? Sadly, not us. They might not even know.

Really the only 100% sure way of finding out is to start working with them. But that is costly when done the traditional way.

How does this all tie back to a board seat? Well most importantly in this context, whether it's an Advisory Board or an Apprenticeship, what we are in fact doing is giving the boards an opportunity to 'try you' before they buy. In both cases you are de-risking a very fraught hiring decision and making it easy for them to say yes. Maybe it works out, maybe it doesn't, but you have managed to get yourself into the inner circle and then it's on you to build from there.

5 components to great investors

Veblen Mantra #3
'If you have money, you can buy any board seat'

1. Connections

Arguably the most important connections you will make in this journey are those with investors. It becomes much easier to build investor conversations as you start investing yourself. You might meet someone at a networking event and they mention they're an investor with a portfolio of companies and a significant Apple holding. That might sound impressive but that could just mean they have $1,000 split across five stocks with $500 of it in Apple. If you're not an investor, you might be impressed without ever understanding the nuance. Anyone can put $100 into a crowdfunding deal and call themselves an angel investor.

To the uninitiated an angel investor might sound impressive. A real investor will want to know more. Your credibility will come from the questions you ask.

As you sit on more boards and take the time to get to know the investors, you will find that if you do a good job of keeping them informed of what is going on, and, ideally, helping them to get good returns, they will start talking to you about other investments they have and other investors you should meet.

You may soon find that investors in one company are asking you to sit on the boards of other companies to represent their interests there. This is the point where you can start to earn significant fees representing those investors.

Whilst other investors, or the people that represent them, are still useful to connect with, it is now the directors of other companies that it is useful to form relationships with. These are the people that will be critical to doing M&A deals.

2. Knowledge

With every step up you take on your board journey you will be presented with new learnings, new ways of doing things.

It is important to build on your knowledge. It is also important to recognise that what works in one type of company won't always work in another, and what works at one size of company won't work at a bigger one. For example, one of the strategic advantages that small companies have is their ability to pivot quickly, to react to customer demand, to innovate, to try things with limited downside risk. With a small team, it is relatively easy to keep everyone on the same page. As you move up to bigger companies with more people, there is much more at risk, more processes are put in place to stop potential catastrophes, and in fact you as a board are there to ensure that the company doesn't accidentally do something dumb.

As the size of your companies and your responsibilities grow, so you need to increase your knowledge in bigger trends. In 2002 I moved to Asia because the largest transfer of wealth in history was moving from West to East and as a young entrepreneur it made sense to be on the receiving end of that migration. Today ESG is a huge trend. Tomorrow baby boomers will transfer their assets to the next generation. AI is in the process of disrupting every industry. Changing climate will lead to mass population changes. And next year something else will be dominating attention.

As a consumer of news these things can be fearful, but thinking like an owner, and connected as you will be, they represent opportunities for you to make a real impact for good. The further up the ladder you get, the more positive impact you can make.

3. Profile

There is a cost to all things. The cost to Elon Musk of his fame is that he cannot go anywhere without guards, but the flip of that is that he can also get on a phone call with nearly anybody on the planet he wants to.

For most of us in business we don't need, or want, that level of fame. But the same principle applies; the better known we become the easier it is to get access to those we want to reach. Additionally the more people who know of us, the more people with potential opportunities will reach out. And the faster we can do deals and get things done. Remember I said business trust is directly related to time?

When we first start updating our LinkedIn profiles we are really accommodating those who will search for us and want proof we are who we say we are. The next level is starting to put ourselves in front of people who don't yet know us. All Veblen members get a PR package as part of the programme which includes third party publishings of podcasts, interviews and thought leadership pieces. But as the size of your influence grows a new opportunity presents itself.

Whilst most people think of PR and communications as a distribution channel to get your voice and ideas out, those that understand it, and choose to play the game, view social media as the ultimate economy with attention as the currency. Once you understand this game, and if you wish to play it, the sky is the limit to how far your influence can spread.

4. Value

As you grow in your role, as your connections, knowledge and influence grow, so too will your understanding of the value you can provide and the worth of that.

You will likely find you turn down more board seats than you accept. As you become a Great Board Member, your interest will only be in roles where you will be challenged but where you know you can meet incredible people and help make maximum impact.

You don't need to be a financial whizz, or a deep-pocketed investor, or an authority on international M&A; you just need to be able to call one at the right time and have them present a solution to your board.

As your reputation for getting stuff done grows, so the people who get stuff done will want to work with you more. This virtuous circle works for everyone and significantly increases the speed to results.

5. Leverage

Leverage at this level has more to do with legacy than boosting your career. There is a reason that so many business leaders we respect ultimately turn to philanthropy. They solve problems in their business, problems in their industry and ultimately look to solve problems in the world.

When you have reached a point where you have incredible resources at your fingertips, not just your personal wealth but companies, organisations and even governments that are willing to work with you, applying those resources to build just another company ceases to offer the intellectual stimulation it once did.

Applying those resources to something truly meaningful can make the biggest difference in your life and those of others less fortunate we share a planet with.

The trick here is not to wait until you have everything ready to get started. Just like your board career, you need to get started before you are ready.

---

1. Bessembinder, Hendrik (Hank) and Chen, Te-Feng and Choi, Goeun and Wei, Kuo-Chiang (John), Long-Term Shareholder Returns: Evidence from 64,000 Global Stocks (March 6, 2023). Financial Analysts Journal, Forthcoming http://dx.doi.org/10.2139/ssrn.3710251

2. S&P 500 Index Fund Average Annual Return Rate: Here's why investing in an S&P 500 index fund could pay off nicely over the long term. Speights, K Nov 13, 2023. https://www.fool.com/investing/how-to-invest-index-funds/average-return/

3. Estimated number of companies worldwide from 2000 to 2021 https://www.statista.com/statistics/1260686/global-companies/#statisticContainer

The great game beyond the game – from Advise to Aware

Advise, Apprentice, Achieve. The levelling up you take as you get more experience, more connections, more knowledge.

Aware is the final level in the game. It is where you really understand all the games that are being played. You don't need a board seat to have control and you can see how 1+1 = 5. It's where you start to play chess with companies to create more value.

You will have a certain detachment from the businesses, but this allows you to see just a little bit into the future so you can position yourself where you need to be.

When Elon Musk or Sir Richard Branson can create multiple billion-dollar businesses across multiple industries, you have to recognise that they are playing at a different level from us mere mortals.

To create a company that gets to $1m in revenue is already pretty special. A $100m company is an achievement that 99% of entrepreneurs will never hit. A $1b company is truly exceptional. To be able to replicate that multiple times in multiple industries suggests a level of insight that is unbelievably rare. And certainly much rarer than the multiple talking heads and journalists (who have never created a business in their lives) explaining everything they think that the CEO is currently doing wrong.

You and I might never reach those lofty heights, but it is important to know they exist. When it comes to dealmaking you are either the one playing or the one being played. It's fine to be played, but make sure you're doing it deliberately.

Structuring deals

Learning how to do M&A (Mergers & Acquisitions) transactions is well beyond the scope of this book, but can be a critical way to add value to boards and grow the companies and shareholder value that you are representing.

Most M&A actually ends up destroying shareholder value because of the vast complexities of trying to merge companies, cultures and systems. If you would like to know how to do it well I suggest you google my business partner Jeremy Harbour who has been teaching small business M&A strategies for nearly twenty years and who has taught me the most on this subject.

How to get the 'dream' board job

I mentioned at the beginning of this book in the disclaimer that this book is designed to get you your first board seat, not your dream board seat.

If you have aspirations of getting a board seat on a Tesla, Coke, IBM or Adidas, you are not going to get that seat through what you learn in these pages. However, there is definitely a clue to it in this investor section.

The fact is that most big company boards do not have a lot of turnover. Decisions about who joins are not made quickly and so your chances of getting a board seat by rocking up and knocking on the door are pretty remote.

Whilst not easy, there is a relatively simple way to get on to the board of a bigger company.

The simplest way to get on to the board of a big company is to have your company acquired by them and make a board seat a condition of ownership.

So, for example, if my objective was a seat on Meta's board, I would have to create a cool tech company. Then I would need to convince them to buy it. Easy, right? No, but I never promised easy.

The way I would do it is to start cannibalising either its members or its advertisers. When I become a big enough pain in their backside it is easier for them to acquire me than fight me, and it is at that point I can sacrifice some of the cash of the purchase for a seat on the board.

There is a slight flaw in this plan of course. Creating a 'cool tech' company big enough to even show up on Meta's radar is a one in a million long shot. If you don't have time to try a million different options, you could potentially fast-track this model by joining the board of a company that is already growing and achieving this. Use outside investors to give you control, keep growing and sacrifice short-term profit for the growth required to annoy Zuck and then be the person that structures that deal, including the seat for you.

But as we will see in the next chapter, if you have already become adept at leveraging board seats to structure multi-million/billion dollar deals, you might discover you actually want to spend less, not more, time in the boardroom.

The boardroom irony. Turning down millions.

And here's the irony. When you get really good at this whole boardroom game, when you have started to fully comprehend the game beyond the game, when you are able to see one, two or more chess moves ahead, then suddenly everyone will be clambering to have you on their boards. And you won't want to sit on any of them.

At that point where you could create the most value, and charge the highest fees, you'll realise that it is much easier just to hire someone else to sit on boards for you to represent your interests, whilst you focus on strategy behind the scenes.

'I guess irony can be pretty ironic sometimes.'
– Buck Murdock (*Airplane II: The Sequel*)

The beginning

The premise of this book was very simply to show you that not only is a board seat achievable for you, it can be a lucrative and constructive way for you to make a real impact in the world.

You may have noticed a theme throughout the book was to 'think like an owner'. This was deliberate. This journey starts and ends with you. So many people that I talk to with regard to the Veblen programme have resisted thinking about board seats in the belief that it won't work for them because they are too old, too young, the wrong gender, colour, industry, job title, not physically able to travel etc.

Hopefully you have seen that it is definitely not impossible. In fact it's very possible.

You now have the blueprint on how to get there. What it needs is for you to take the first steps. To do something each day!

The Boardroom Blueprint is a simple but effective way to get on to the board ladder and use it to significantly enhance your career. Like anything, although it might be simple it requires work. As you'll have read it is relatively easy to use these techniques to get your first board seat, but it is on you to do a good job once you have the role.

That desire to do a good job can only come from you. Fortunately if you have taken the time to read this far, then I'm guessing you are someone committed to learning and growing, and that is the most important thing.

As you've seen from some of the stories shared, there is nothing holding you back. What you currently see as your biggest disadvantage may actually be of the biggest value to the right board.

As promised, I'm going to include some gifts to help you on your journey. The gifts are to ensure you don't procrastinate on what I believe will be the most game-changing, career-altering action you can take. People procrastinate for two reasons.

1. They don't know the next step

2. They are afraid of the results

In this Board Pack for you at , you will find a version of the 'first 30 day' challenge that our members work through. Although some of you will get your first board seat in those thirty days, most will find it builds the foundation you need so that over the next thirty days you can start to have the really important conversations to secure that first seat or seats.

I'm also going to include a bunch of other goodies that I've mentioned throughout the book.

You have the tools; you have the blueprint. No more excuses.

Now where were we in the board meal?

***

Back in the restaurant, the sound of slightly raised voices from your table snaps your mind back to the task in hand. Even a year ago, hearing board members arguing like this would have made you anxious, but by now you know the parties involved, you know who is playing games because they enjoy the drama, who is arguing but for the wrong reasons and who is the individual that actually has the real control and could potentially derail things if they are pushed too hard.

As the slightly tense voices die down, you remind everybody to put personal preferences aside and focus on what is best for all shareholders in the long term. However, you know that the information you are about to share with them will make the previous discussion redundant. You also know it will make everyone at the table and many of the company's staff very, very wealthy.

For full effect you had planned to wait until dessert, but it seems like now is as good a time as any. You tap your wine glass and rise to your feet.

'Esteemed colleagues,' you begin. 'For several years we have run a successful Board Apprentice Programme and we're lucky enough to be joined by several of the members tonight.' Murmurs of appreciation ripple around the table and a couple of glasses are raised in the general direction of the Apprentices. 'What you might not know,' you continue, 'is that one of them has been very successfully sharing our business story with investors around the world. I have had several conversations with new investors over the past few months as a direct result of this, and we've all seen an appreciable nudge in share price despite the wider market malaise. One of those investors, a large private equity player with an excellent reputation, has recently reached ownership of 4.9% of our company and over the past few days I have met with the CEO and CIO in person to discuss where they would like to go with us in the future.

'What I'm about to pass around to all members of this board is...'

You pause for dramatic effect and look around the room slowly. 'A formal letter of intent to buy out the remaining shares in our company at a 33% premium to today's closing price and take us private again.'

You scan the room again watching the wave of emotions cross the different board members' faces. You know some were already happily calculating what this did to their net worths. The exec directors were trying to figure out what this would mean for their teams. Other directors, those with fewer shares, were wondering whether they would still have jobs at the end of it.

'Before I open this up for discussion, let me remind you of the highly sensitive nature of this topic and that any leaks, whilst illegal, would also likely kill this deal. This offer has come very suddenly, but both the key executives are in town and wanted to present to the board tomorrow. So I would like to propose we postpone board items 1–6 tomorrow and listen instead to them articulate their plan and their vision for our company. There will be no formal vote tomorrow, but if both parties are happy we will look to move to vote and announce by the end of the month.'

You sit back down and wait for the shock to subside and the questions to start. Having been involved in these discussions for most of the last forty-eight hours you already know this proposal would get the votes it needed and had already worked out exactly what this would do for your net worth.

And to think that it had all started with a book...

Questions and answers from early readers

What are the legal risks?

A director of a company does take or legal responsibility for the decisions of that company. This is not to be taken lightly. An Advisory Board member or an Apprentice takes on no such legal risk which makes it a great place to start.

When you join the board of a PLC you should always ensure that the company has D&O insurance (Directors and officers liability insurance) which gives you some protection in the event that the directors are sued.

What other risks are there?

Reputational is probably the biggest. f you join a company and that company gets into trouble, even if you are protected legally, it might not be great for your personal brand.

The board of Theranos (Silicon Valley blood testing start-up that turned out to be a fraud) suffered much reputational damage.

However, this shouldn't be something that holds you back at the beginning of your board career.

How much time does being a board member take?

I've sat on boards that for long periods of time have not taken more than a couple of hours a month including reading and calls. I've sat on others that have had periods where I've had to work round the clock to sort problems out.

In most cases you're looking at a couple of hours of meetings a month, plus half a day's reading. Each company is different. The more value you want to add, the more time you will likely contribute.

Where can I find out more about the Veblen Programme?

Go to VeblenDirectors.com and book a call with one of our lovely team. I also recommend you subscribe to our YouTube channel and follow us on LinkedIn. We post lots of content that you can repost on your own feed to build your boardroom credentials.

Where can I see more case studies of people and their board journeys?

https://www.youtube.com/@VeblenDirectors

And

https://www.linkedin.com/company/veblen-director-programme

Should I get a director's certificate or qualification?

If you really want to, but real-world board experience is far more valuable than certificates. As we've discussed in this book, a genuine curiosity and desire to help (soft skills) are actually far more valuable when you're starting out. As you move into bigger companies, if you feel a certification would help, go for it, but it's definitely not required and won't significantly help you get a seat.

What is a good size for a board?

When a company is small, less is definitely more; you want decisions to be made quickly. Three to five is probably optimum. As the company grows, it can (but not always) be useful to add numbers. Always strive for odd numbers to avoid deadlocks.

Should boards be about discussions or decisions?

In general I find it is better to circulate ideas ahead of the board meeting, let people bounce questions around in an online forum and then just use the board meeting for final clarifications and voting.

This keeps board meetings sharp and to the point, and also means there should be no surprises.

You should always know the way the vote will go before you walk into the boardroom.

Can I only get a board seat in my country?

No, please start thinking globally!

Do I need to buy stock in the company?

Whilst this is a lovely gesture of support and will send a very positive message to the market it is not necessary. Often as part of your compensation you will receive stock and this can be very lucrative if the share price is rising.

What about conflicts of interest with my current company?

Try to avoid it at all costs. There are lots of companies out there, no need to antagonise your own company or open yourself up to any suggestions of proprietary.

What is the difference between private and public companies for board members?

Mostly the level of scrutiny you're under. If you want to see how bad it can get, you can read my previous book Entrepreneurial Investing. PLCs typically have more investors, and that means more demands on the business. It's great when it's going well, but can be tough if the share price is declining.

In the US, which is highly litigious, this can also lead to lots of lawsuits which are never fun.

Some of our Veblen members join private boards as a stepping stone and then decide they are happy to stay private. But if you really want to hit the big leagues, PLCs are where it's at.

Can this *really* be achieved in 60 days?!

Absolutely. There will be some people who won't even have finished this book, before they will have realised exactly who in their network they needed to talk to and how to pitch them. Several Veblen members have done this within days of joining and realising how they could add value to boards.

For others they feel they need to 'get their ducks in a row' and want to update their profiles and do some more learning before they reach out. But if you follow the process laid out in this book and come at it from the angle of helping a business out, rather than furthering your own personal goals, then there is absolutely no reason why within a month or two from now you can't be updating your LinkedIn profile with 'board member'

Get your copy of The Boardroom Blueprint Board Pack

https://boardroom-blueprint.com/boardpack/

When you come to claim your Board Pack, you will receive the following:

- Links to our Boardroom Quizzes.

- My interview with Darren Finkelstein on how to get the accountability you need for your goals and some great tips for holding others accountable.

- Interview with Victoria Sylvester who is one of the foremost experts on ESG in the small cap markets and who perfectly balances values with capitalist realities.

- Veblen founding member Mirenda Canady shares a simple and very successful way to reach out to founders and secure your first board seat.

- You'll get the .pdf download 'I've got a board seat, now what?' which you will need as soon as you get your first board seat.

- A $500 voucher to be used on any Veblen course.

- A $500 voucher you can send to a friend.

- Access to the Veblen Community Group.

- A video I put together on how we now approach small cap equities to better control some of the challenges of the public markets.

A final word from Callum Laing

I've talked briefly about my time working in a big, successful company. I worked very hard, made good money and had a lot of fun. When I first came to Asia and started building companies I worked much harder, made no money and had very little fun. What had changed? The environment. Not being in Asia, but being in a business being run by someone who didn't understand how to run a business. Me.

There was an idea that I kept coming back to, but yet couldn't really figure out what to do with. When I was at University, I started a rowing club; we secured some Lottery funds, bought some boats and over two years built a very successful novice rowing club. As one of the few people in the club who had ever rowed before I was one of the best and enjoyed helping others to learn.

One summer I went home and was invited to race in a senior open crew. For those not familiar, a novice crew is like playing footy with your mates at the weekend. Senior Open is like playing in the premiership. There is a big difference.

Now I say I was 'invited' and that's the way I like to remember it, but if I'm honest what happened was someone dropped out, the next fifty people they tried were unavailable and I happened to be available. I was stuck in the bow (front) of the boat where I could do the least damage and was told to 'Keep up and don't "mess" up' (or words to that effect but slightly more threatening).

Fortunately we won our first race and so I ended up rowing with them quite a lot over the summer. Naturally I was terrified and did everything I could to keep up and not 'mess up'. Two things became very obvious the more I rowed with them. The first was that because everyone else in the boat was better than me, I did not have to compensate for anyone else and could focus 100% on my own stroke. I could also copy those that were better than me. This meant that I personally improved more in that month or two as a rower than I had done in the previous few years. The second thing I noticed was that even when we weren't pulling at 100% we were still travelling much, much faster than any boat I had ever rowed in before.

Although I didn't always have the choice it convinced me that I always wanted to be on teams that had stronger players than me.

Bringing this back to my struggling start-up, I knew that I was clearly not in a winning team, but I couldn't figure out how you surround yourself with better people, especially when you don't have the funds to hire them. I started inviting better entrepreneurs for monthly lunches, and they inadvertently became my first 'Advisory Board'.

Over the years I did start to work it out and I realised that starting a business and hoping good people come to you is a long shot. Surrounding yourself with good people and then starting a business was a much better approach. Advisory Boards became my way of doing that.

When I set up Veblen I wanted to provide an environment where our members always had people a few steps ahead of them on the journey that they could go to to learn from. I wanted to provide for them an environment like that Senior Open rowing boat. High degrees of accountability, but enough great people around them that they could learn from others and improve. And the more people join and do that the higher the standard becomes for all. And even if they are not all pulling at 100% you still reach the destination quicker.

If you're interested in joining that community, I do hope you'll reach out. Putting yourself in the right environment can solve many problems.

See you in the boardroom!

Thanks

Part of the reason Connections is the first of the repeatable steps is that you need to be deliberate about surrounding yourself with people that will hold you to a higher standard, that can inspire you, that you can learn from. I don't consider it the most important thing.   consider it everything.

If you take nothing else from this book other than that, I hope you become deliberate about the people you surround yourself with on your path to success.

In the following pages are just some of the people that I owe a massive debt of thanks to for inspiring me to greater things.

To my family; Zo, Mia and Ella keep me grounded, laughing and inspired.

To my business partners and friends Jeremy Harbour and Victor Tan that keep the engine running.

To Franzi, John and more recently Michelle for leading Veblen forward.

The team alongside them: Jon, Pam Rene, Yanni, RC, Markieta, Germaine, Sheeraline, Danny and Shruti.

Extra special thanks to Shruti for the book cover!

Plus all the experts who so generously donate their time to help Veblen members.

To the Unity dealmakers: Charlotte, Muriel, Susan, Wayne, Alex, Jerriel, Jess, Dinnah, Sam and Paul.

To my case studies: Marisa Agrasut, Ralph White and the amazing Vikki Sylvester who has served alongside me on the board for many years.

To my own accountability buddies and brains trust: Martin Jimmink, Ian Grundy, Daniel Priestley and Paul Dunn.

To Debs Jenkins and Lisa for whipping this book into shape.

To all the other board members I've sat alongside over the years. I've learnt from you all – even if the lessons weren't easy to swallow. Many thanks.

And to all the Veblen founding members who inspire me every day:

Cheng Bee, Michael, Marisa, Patrick, Ralph, Kristy, Angela, Punit, Paul, Hetul, AJ, Lenka, Jim, Vincent, David, John, Dr. Veronica, Kayode, Jeremy, Martin, Chandra, David, David, Anthony, Vijay, Anandi, Arvashni, Kawaljeet, Cameron, Jonathan, Uldis, Nam Phong, Ronawati, Ifrah, Irene, Tokeshia, Diane, Scott, Mark, Paul, Padmini, Pamela, Ryan, Kellie, Jeremy, Bernard, Mirenda, Paul, Erin, Payal, Gwarega, Nomonde, Mazen, Camelia, Susan, Glenn, Claudio, Sibusiso, Ramesh, Sashidar, Oluwafemi, Adam, Andreas, Zafer, Sandra, Keith, Adedamola, Adrian, Mark, Mauricio, Mohamed Munaf, Rafik, Seth, Sekai, Mohammed, Scott, Ayo, Cassie, Indira, Christophe, Vineet, Brendon, Valerie, Brad, Graham, Mike, Chaitalee, Corina, Shantanu, Michel, Ray, Daniel, David, Sanjay, Peggy, Hiromi, Srinivasa(Nivas), Namrata, Edward, Michelle, Rishi, Anand, Karim, Lex, Ferdie, Rachit, Jean Noel, James, Jan-Philipp, Claire, Francisco, Viktoriya, Marc, Sanjay, Rick, David, Anjali, Tibor, William and Suresh.

'You're still here? It's over. Go home.'

– Ferris Bueller

Other books by Callum Laing

More Praise for Boardroom Blueprint

'Boardroom Blueprint' is a masterclass in leadership and strategic thinking. It's a trove of inspiration and practical wisdom, truly feeding the ambitions of those who aspire to pave their way to the boardroom. It's a five-star read, focusing on empowering its readers.

– Aladdin Abdulkareem, Portfolio Manager, Interactive Brokers

Incredible! This guide is the ultimate roadmap for securing a board seat. It's not only thorough and all-encompassing but also engaging and actually a fun read. Who would've thought?

– Scott Friedman, Global Speaking Fellow, Founder/CEO 'Together We Can Change the World'

It's about time that the traditional boardroom was shaken up! Quite simply, if you want to be an effective board member, you have to read this book and apply the lessons.

– Nick Bradley, CEO & Founder, High Value Exit

The path to joining your first board can seem formidable, but 'Boardroom Blueprint' is not just a book; it's a mentor in print form. Callum lays out a clear plan with actionable steps, demystifying the process and showing you exactly how to close the gap between ambition and your next big career achievement.

– Erika Lafrenrie, Managing Partner at Luminae Group

Some books are packed with useful information, some are easy to read. Few are both - this is one of the few.

– Jeremy King, Managing Director, King Campbell & Friends

Callum advocates upholding strong values, acting with integrity, and aiming to uplift companies and causes you serve. This book provides a clear framework and actionable strategies for aspiring board members.

– Jess Jeetley MBE, Founder CEO, Bot Theory

As a comprehensive and insightful journey into the world of board membership, 'Boardroom Blueprint' is a standout choice. It masterfully blends the author's decades of real-world experience with a narrative that is both engaging and instructive.

– Rear Admiral Sanjay Roye, Chief Staff Officer (Strategic Operations) & Chief Staff Officer (Personnel and Administration), Indian Navy

Never have I ever read a book that has energised me, and had a 'call-to-action' like 'Boardroom Blueprint'.

– Robert Mazibuko, Managing Director

Callum Laing's 'Boardroom Blueprint' is a personal and empathetic guide, weaving entertainment with profound insights into a concise and accessible roadmap for leadership. In a crowded landscape, Laing's decision to share this invaluable resource reflects his deep understanding of our challenges in the boardroom.

– Bhada Sinhaphalin, Founder, Chom Living

www.ingramcontent.com/pod-product-compliance
Lightning Source LLC
Chambersburg PA
CBHW041209220326
41597CB00030BA/5203